LOVI'
HARD
When They're Hard to Love

ESSAYS ON RAISING TEENS
IN TODAY'S COMPLEX, CHAOTIC WORLD

WHITNEY FLEMING

To my mom,
for showing me the power of a mother's love.

To Payton, Olivia & Camryn,
for forgiving all my mistakes and letting me grow up
alongside you.

To Mark,
for loving me through it all.

Contents

PREFACE

I'm not a parenting expert. I'm not a trained psychologist or mental health therapist or life coach.

I'm a mom.

A parent who loves her kids more than life itself. My guess is if you're reading this book, you are too.

I love being a mother, but I'm not always good at it. I've made a lot of mistakes. I still do.

I'm currently launching three teenage girls into this complicated world.

This is hard.

The system for raising teenagers in our modern times sets us up for failure. It's easy to feel that everyone else seems to have it all together while you sit and cry in the high school parking lot. Self-proclaimed experts give contradictory information that is irrelevant when your teenager is a different person each day. And we don't want to admit that we are worried we're not doing it right, that we don't know what we're doing, or that there are times we don't want to do it at all.

We feel alone because no one wants to highlight their kid's screw-ups on social media. No one talks about their poor decisions at curriculum night. No one wants to admit that you may have messed up this parenting gig. No one wants to make their teen a target or have them judged.

We are left floating in murky, shark-infested, unchartered waters, drowning in a sea of teenage angst.

But it's not just the brutal that makes it an emotional roller coaster; it's also all the overwhelmingly beautiful things occurring. It's watching your teenager find their passions, take charge of their newfound independence, and move on to a new chapter. It's carving out a new, more mature relationship. It's letting go of a beautiful kite and watching it soar off into the sky.

It's an impossible paradox to understand until you are sitting on the crossroads – clinging to 'what was' while launching them into 'what's next' and always wondering if you did enough.

And through it all, we ask ourselves: *"Am I the only one who feels this way?"*

GROWING UP, THEM AND ME

One day, after what seemed like the millionth argument I had with one of my pre-teen daughters, I broke down and cried.

I did not have the relationship I wanted with her. In fact, I barely had a relationship at all.

I felt guilty for not giving her a better parent, one who would know how to handle these tween and teen years better.

But mostly, it seemed like I was the only one who was struggling to get along with their kids.

So, I realized I had a choice. I could muddle through these years hoping that we would come out on the other side; or, I could do something about it.

I decided if I wanted a better relationship with my kids, I had to work on myself first.

I had to understand my own triggers that caused me to be angry and irrational.

I needed to deal with my own past issues and relationships.

I focused on developing coping mechanisms for stress, anxiety and fear of the unknown.

I separated out their behavior and choices from my own, placing my expectations to the side.

I found that when I felt in charge of my emotions and confident in my choices, I could be the parent my kids needed instead of feeling like their behavior was a reflection on me.

I yelled less. I connected more. I gave space. I gave grace.

I tried to understand the *why* behind their behavior instead of focusing on *how* it impacted me.

I focused on being grateful for the small things my kids did and formed an unconditional belief in their goodness.

I continued to address my own issues, like my anxious nature, my personal insecurities and how to turn my empathy into compassion.

I learned to lean into the qualities I did not like about my kids at the time and love harder. We all grew up, together, a little more every day.

It wasn't easy. It wasn't pretty.

But it started with me. And things slowly got better.

Our relationship isn't perfect, but it's a beautiful work in progress. A preamble to what I hope to be a long story of connection to my kids throughout their life.

YEARS FILLED WITH STORIES

What follows on these pages is a series of essays I've written about finding myself while raising my big kids.

As children grow up, parents stop talking about the struggles, and many feel completely alone and overwhelmed with the challenges facing today's adolescents. Desperate to maintain a connection to their evolving child, often they don't need advice as much as someone who encourages them to keep going – and reassures them it's going to be okay.

That is what I hope this book is for you.

I'm not here to offer expert advice. Instead, I hope it brings some peace to the parent who feels ostracized, clarity to what's important in parenting tweens and teens, and affirms that there is no one path to launch our kids successfully into the world.

I hope that no matter what you are going through with your child, it encourages you to love them harder, even when – especially when – they are hard to love.

SECTION 1:

THESE TEENAGE YEARS WILL BREAK YOU

INTRODUCTION

A friend texted me recently. "How do our teens know how to hit us exactly where it hurts?" I thought about it for a second, and my only reply was: "Because they aren't stupid. They just do and say dumb things sometimes."

And it's so odd that this person you would give your life for can cause such complex emotions. They will blame you for all their problems.

They will say that you are too strict or too controlling or put too much pressure on them or that you didn't push them enough.

They can make you feel like an idiot.

They will make bad choices, wrong choices, that you know deep down aren't your fault. Somehow you will still believe it's your fault.

They will break your rules.

They will break your trust.

They will break your heart with their words, with their actions, with a single stare.

Some problems will be bigger than others. They will all feel like big problems.

People will tell you to pick and choose your battles. Sometimes it's hard to choose when there are so many battles.

I know kids make mistakes. I know children will disappoint. I know it is all about the process of growing up and letting go.

But knowing this still doesn't prepare you for the surge of emotions you feel when it happens to you.

I wonder, where did I go wrong? Or, I thought we had a better relationship than this.

But mostly I think, *Wow, I am really screwing this up.*

Everyone will tell you to enjoy every second because it goes by so fast. You will be caught in the middle of wanting time to slow down and to get through this challenging phase a little faster.

You won't tell anyone these things, because you don't want to look like a jerk.

You wonder if anyone else feels this way. Does anyone else struggle with their relationship with their teenager? Does anyone else lose sleep?

Does anyone else's heart feel shattered into a million tiny pieces scattered on the floor?

You are tired, *so tired*, of the fighting and the blaming and the judging.

You want to celebrate all the beautiful moments, because there are so many beautiful moments.

But you also want to pull away to protect yourself, to protect your heart that has given so much. It's tempting to walk away, to throw your hands up in the air, and give up.

But instead, I choose to lean in, I choose to move toward the pain and the betrayals of trust and the mistakes. I choose to relinquish control of how their choices reflect on me.

I choose to forgive again and again and start over each day.

I choose to focus on the growth and the learning and the achievements, however small or large they may be.

And instead of speaking my emotions, I choose words from my broken heart: "No matter what you do, dear child of mine, no matter the mistakes you make, the goals you achieve, there is nothing you can do to make me love you any more or any less."

Because I have to believe that with every action, with every mean-spirited word, with every effort my teens use to push me away, they want me – they need me – to be there for them, no matter what.

While I still may feel angry or disappointed or frustrated, I find other people to share those feelings with, so eventually, I can give my teens the love they need – and the consequences to know they must be accountable in this life.

And we keep talking and trying to navigate this growing-up thing together – and in those moments, my heart starts to piece itself back together again, if only just a little bit.

This stage of parenting is breathtakingly beautiful and intensely painful at the same time. It is a jumbled combination of pride and astonishment and chaos and worry.

I want more than to just get through this challenging phase of parenting, but today, that is my goal.

Step by step. One intense day at a time.

And I can only hope that as I begin to let go and send my kids out into this world, as they take the lessons I've taught to craft a place for themselves – an even more beautiful life will come to fruition for my kids than I could have ever imagined.

And I want to be a part of it.

So I keep forging ahead.

I wish I could say this rough road for my kids and me is almost over, but in truth, I know we are in the thick of it.

I keep trying to develop tough skin while keeping a tender heart.

Because my teens may keep breaking my heart, but I know it's big enough to carry us all through this journey.

And I want to see what's on the other side.

1. THESE TEENAGE YEARS WILL BREAK YOU

The teenage years will break you.

It will test your resolve, your patience, your parenting choices.

It will make you feel lonely and ostracized when you're the only parent saying 'no'.

It will make you feel insignificant and unworthy when your teenager lashes out.

It will make you wonder how one person can have so much laundry.

It will make you feel broken and lost when you can't seem to get your kid back on track. It will test your ability to keep your mouth shut when you need to pick and choose your battles. You will feel like your head may explode when you walk past their room.

It will test your ability to forgive when your teenager messes up – which they will, over and over again.

It will make you wonder where you went wrong.

It will make you feel helpless as you watch your kid face a world so much more complicated than the one we grew up in just two decades ago.

It will test your nerves as you watch them hop into a car or go on a trip or even a date, leaving you to feel helpless and unable to protect them.

It will make you feel weak and feeble when you can't help them quash their anxiety about school or relationships or how they will survive in this tough world.

It will make you bone-tired from driving and worry and worry and driving.

It will make you feel the weight of guilt so heavy it crushes you.

Yes, these challenging teenage years will break you.

You'll smile all day when your teenage daughter surprisingly pecks you on the cheek before she leaves for school or drop everything you're doing because your son asked you to watch a video on his phone, your two heads almost touching looking at the small screen.

Your heart will burst with happiness when you hear how kind they've been to a stranger.

You'll find yourself challenged to look at the world in new ways because of their budding idealism.

You'll feel unabashed pride as they find their passions, finish their education, start chasing their dreams.

You'll see glimpses of the person they are becoming, and you begin to look forward to seeing what they will do with their life.

You will learn to accept change, because there is no turning back.

You'll learn that any communication is good communication, so you'll figure out emojis and snaps and Instagram.

You will buy the best snacks so they'll want to bring their friends over, and you'll spend your last dollar at Starbucks just to get a few extra moments in the car with them.

You will sneak into their room some nights, and they will still be awake. But as they are lying in their bed scrolling through their phone or finishing homework or listening to music, for a brief moment, you'll see that toddler face again, and your heart will break into pieces.

And then, when they look up at you with sleepy eyes as you kiss them on the forehead and, if you are very fortunate, they say something like, "I love you too," you'll sleep easy that night.

Yes, these teenage years will break you in every way, but if you're lucky, you've raised people who will help put you back together again.

2. Did I Do Enough?

You will always wonder if you did enough.

You will always wish that you had one more opportunity to scoop them up when they fall, hugging them to your chest to help the pain go away.

You will always want one more morning of early cartoons snuggled on the couch, one more bath where the whole room gets wet, one more holiday where they believed – really believed – in the magic.

You will always long for just one more opportunity to get it right, to soak up their littleness, to love them perfectly.

But you can't turn back time.

So you look at the lovely adult-sized children in front of you, and you sigh with the acceptance that one part of your life is over, and another beautiful chapter is beginning.

And your desire to go back turns into hope.

You hope they believed you all those times you told them how proud they should be of themselves.

You hope you gave them the confidence to say 'no' to the wrong things, but more importantly, to say 'yes' to the right ones.

You hope they understand that they have value, they have so much potential, they are worthy – of respect, of consideration, of so much love.

You hope they look back on their childhood and remember the laughter, the traditions, the warmth, and they forget when you yelled, when you were frustrated, when you were spent.

You hope they are ready. You hope you did enough.

Because they let go of your hand more and more – and they are almost ready to launch out into this world, even if you are not.

As I watch this final transformation into beautiful butterflies waiting to take flight, I silently will them at each and every moment to look back at me, if only for just a second.

And see me waiting there with my hands and heart wide open, just in case they need to grab on to something steady while they start to soar.

You'll always wonder if you did enough.

You'll always hope they are ready.

You'll always be there for them as long as you have breath in your body and a beating heart filled with love.

These are the things I know.

3. RAISING TEENS IS BLOODY CHAOS

Since my parenting gig began nearly 17 years ago, I have felt overwhelmed.

I started off with twin girls born five weeks premature and then added a third daughter sixteen months later.

Chasing three kids around close in age is both joyous and stressful.

At one point, I changed roughly 30 diapers and washed about 25 bottles and sippy cups every single day. My life was consumed with hoisting little ones onto my hips and cleaning up toy rooms and laundry – oh, so much laundry.

And at the end of each night, I would collapse into my bed physically exhausted, spent, and unsure if I could do it again the following day.

As the pandemonium of living with three toddlers transformed into raising school-aged kids,

I finally found my groove. Our life was still hectic but in a controlled way. I felt satisfied with our life and how we lived it.

And then my kids turned into tweens and teens.

I was not prepared for what happened next.

To put it simply, it's bloody chaos. I had no idea how mentally exhausting the teenage years would be.

While my kids continue to become more independent, there is so much to remember.

It's driving my kids to school early and picking them up late. It's fundraisers, school projects and homecoming dress shopping.

It's orthodontist appointments, sports physicals and weekends out of town for tournaments.

It's thinking about college while trying to let them be kids. It's helping them discover who they are while trying to keep them safe.

It's constant trips to the grocery store because there are always kids at my house, forgetting it's my turn for carpool and the terror of teaching them to drive and laundry – still. so. much. laundry.

In between, I desperately try to carve out family time so I can remember what my kids look like.

But more than the remembering, there's the worrying.

It's the drugs that are most definitely in my kids' schools, the cyberbullying and the academic pressures.

It's the requests I hear about for nude selfies and violence at every corner.

It's alcohol at every social gathering and phones glued to hands.

It's tough decisions about dating and sleepovers and school trips and where they want to 'hang out'.

It is exhausting trying to bite my tongue, choose my battles and let my daughters have some independence.

It's ignoring some eye-rolls and epic sighs and snarky teen remarks.

It's closing the door on messy rooms and accepting that sometimes I can't fix their world, no matter how much I want to do precisely that.

And it is lonely.

When all your kids are gone from sunrise to sunset and the peace and quiet you so desperately sought a decade before feels ominous and heavy.

It's wondering who you can talk to when your kid makes a bad decision.

It's feeling like you are the only one who has a bad relationship with your teen.

It's trying to figure out where the time went and trying not to think about the time you have left when you're all under one roof.

So, I stress about consciously enjoying every last orchestra concert and game and movie where we all sit close together on our couch.

I lament at how fast the time streaked by. I'm sad when I can no longer kiss a *boo-boo* or carry my child upstairs after a long day.

In all this, I often find that I am mentally drained at the end of each day, and I collapse into my bed as I did in those early years.

And while I am exhausted, I am still so in awe and wonder and love for those three babies that somehow never let me sleep peacefully.

I never expected the teenage years to be this exhausting.

It's a roller coaster, but totally worth the ride.

It is exciting to watch my kids grow in their passions.

I am so proud of their every success.

I am hopeful that they will bring light into this dark world and can't wait to see what they accomplish next.

I celebrate their spirit, determination and yes, even their missteps.

Nothing else in life gets simultaneously easier and harder at the same time.

I was not mentally prepared for how exhausting it would be during the teenage years, but oh what a wonderful ride it is.

4. You Will Feel Like You Are Losing Them

You can feel like you are losing them during the teenage years, even though they're right there in front of you.

One day, you are laughing and getting along, the next, you feel like you are sitting with a stranger you don't know in the least.

They might be unrecognizable, growing six inches in a span of six months.

They might have changed personalities, from sweet and loving to salty and stoic.

They might have changed their interests, their focus, their dreams.

You lose them to their phones. You lose them to their rooms. You lose them to their friends, their activities, their jobs.

You may feel desperate to cling to the child you once knew, the one who adored you, the one you got along with, the one whose hand you thought you'd hold forever.

You may feel like crying from their constant rejection. You may feel lost when you can't get them back on track. You may feel insignificant when they ignore you or lash out.

You will grow impatient with the status of your relationship. You will feel frustrated with the push and pull. You will grieve what is no longer there.

You will pull back. You will say less. You will watch from afar.

You will take whatever interaction you can get, even if it is always on their terms.

You will pick and choose your battles because you are tired of so many battles.

You will try to stay available even though they are mostly unavailable.

And then one day, when you least expect it, you will feel something shift.

You'll see glimpses of the person they are becoming, and you begin to look forward to seeing what they will do with their life.

You start to learn about their new interests, their new passions, their new sense of self.

You will begin building a new relationship, one where you are no longer their sun. Your job is to be their moon, connected by a force so strong that it will never break. You will follow them along, providing light in their darkest moments, direction when needed. Sometimes your presence is large and looming, and sometimes it is small, barely seen by the naked eye. But you will always be there.

It won't be perfect. It won't be what it was.

But if you can survive losing your teen for a little bit, what happens when they come back to you can be even more beautiful.

5. The Time Went to Love

Sometimes I look at them, and I wonder where did the time go?

I panic for a moment, almost losing my breath because it all went so fast.

And the longing to go back in time is so strong that I feel the pain in my chest.

How did they grow up so fast, did we make enough memories, where did the time go?

And in the next second, the next inhale in, I remember.

It went to thousands of bedtime stories and giggles under the covers and desperate searches for *lovies* that were lost in their messy rooms.

It went to pounds of apples and peanut butter while watching a show on our living room floor and learning how to ride bicycles and making s'mores on warm summer nights.

It went to worrying if they were sick or did they have friends that cared or was I going to be late picking them up from school.

It went to snuggles on the couch, watching movies they picked with little hands and eating ice cream sundaes that ended up on their shirts and Sunday night dinners where we sat around the table laughing at how silly their dad was that night.

It went to hours in the car going to school events and lessons and sports practices in the rain and cold.

It went to wiping away tears when they fell down on the rough concrete and giving hugs when things didn't go their way and having hard conversations about friendships.

It went to sitting in dark parking lots waiting for their bus to return and traveling hours to watch them perform and baking cakes at 10:30 p.m. for no reason at all.

Sometimes I look at these beautiful creatures who make me so proud, so frustrated, so desperate to hang on to the past, that I forget to see what truly is in front of me.

Where did the time go?

It went to love – more love than I ever thought one person could have in her heart.

And that is time well spent.

6. Stay on Their Path

There are times when raising teenagers that no matter what you do, your relationship still isn't what you want it to be.

You give space, you give grace.

You pick and choose your battles.

You encourage and try to set reasonable boundaries.

You love them at their worst and stay available.

You say yes whenever you can, and no to keep them safe.

You show interest in their interests, you show up to all the things.

You listen, you love, you keep trying.

Yet still, there is a distance between you; still, there is tension; still, it does not feel right.

And even when you've been down this road before, each and every day the path is covered with something new, making it harder and harder to find your way back to a time when you were close to your child, harder to be in a place you both find comfortable and warm.

When you've done all you can to make it work, and yet it still isn't working, there are only a few choices.

You can give up, push back, or keep trudging forward, knowing you may lose control for a while.

You continue walking, even though you have no idea what lies on the path in front of you.

So today, I surrender to the fact that although my relationship doesn't look the way I want it to, that our growing pains may hurt a little more than others, I have to believe that teens come back to their mothers.

I know this because I was once a teen daughter, too. Almost overnight, I went from feeling like my mother was always breathing down my neck to her becoming one of my dearest friends and confidants.

It's hard for me to imagine now, and it's hard for me to remember, but I know in my heart it's true.

And I dig deep for patience, and I dig deep not to force our relationship, and I dig deep to let her go even though all I want to do is hold on as tight as I can.

While she continues to walk farther in front of me to sever the last remaining strings of our bond, I silently hold on to the few I have left.

And I cling to the hope that one day, not too far off in the future, my teen will find her path back to me, where I will be waiting with open arms.

Because no matter how hard the road is between us, how treacherous the terrain, how I might lose control, I'll be on it every step of the way.

7. Raising Teens Is Easy-Peasey

I have no idea why people say raising teenagers is so hard. It's really quite simple.

You just need to make sure you let them have their independence, but also have a strong set of rules and boundaries.

You need to supervise their education but don't interfere too much. Check the parent portal, but not too much. Ensure your child is doing their schoolwork, but not too much. Grades aren't that important, but make sure they are trying their best.

Monitor what your teen is doing online, but don't invade their privacy. Keep up with all the latest trends on YouTube and TikTok and Snapchat and every app that comes out each day. Set appropriate screen time limits even though most of their schooling is now online.

Stay involved with your teen but let them fail.

Pick and choose your battles, but not that battle. Not that one either. Maybe that battle, but you won't know until later if you picked the right one.

Spend quality time with your teenager, but don't force them to spend time with you. Don't worry if they never want to spend time with you. That's normal.

Teenagers absolutely need their sleep. Good luck getting them to go to bed. Or getting them out of bed in the morning. Also note, teens need to learn to get themselves out of bed in the morning and put themselves to bed at night.

Nutrition is super important, so make sure your teen has access to fruits and vegetables, but also don't make what they eat a big deal. Ignore the 47 empty bags of Takis you found in their backpack and encourage healthy choices. Sour Patch Kids are practically a fruit.

Give your teen loads of grace, but also hold them accountable. Just make sure you are picking and choosing the right battles.

Keep talking to your kids about sex, drugs, social issues, online dangers, what to do in an active shooter situation, consent, their future, the environment, etc. Let them do the talking. It's normal if they don't want to talk to you.

Make sure they are kind but know how to stand up for themselves. Teach them to respect authority but not succumb to it. Raise independent thinkers but don't let them get too extreme. Learn how to fight for causes they believe in, but don't ruffle too many feathers.

Make sure they are well-rounded by participating in activities but also ensure they have plenty of downtime.

Don't take your teen's attitude personally. Remember, you're the grown-up. But don't beat yourself up when you don't act like the grown-up. You're only human. Give yourself grace.

Love your kid exactly as they are, but make sure not to raise a jerk. Model good behavior even when your kid never wants to come out of their room. Make sure to spend quality time, but respect their privacy.

Encourage them to discover who they are but never comment on their clothing, hair, significant other, friends, activities, or any choice you disagree with at any time.

Try to enjoy every moment, even when your teen makes it hard.

Why does it always feel hard when it looks so easy for everyone else?

Oh yeah, don't forget to pick and choose your battles, but after you've picked one, you'll probably realize you chose the wrong one. Again.

Don't worry too much.

The kids will be fine as long as you do your best. Stay available and on their terms, but not too available. Don't let them walk all over you.

All they need is love. And rules. And independence. And boundaries. And resilience. And confidence. And humility. And manners. And money. Lots of money.

And an education, unless they don't want an education. Then they should find a trade but make sure you don't push them in a certain direction. Make sure you let them chase their dreams but in a realistic way. Don't worry if they don't know what they want to do with their life but make sure they get a job out of college.

Help them, but don't enable them. Support them, but don't coddle them. Be there, but make sure you're not there too much.

And also: don't put so much pressure on yourself. You're doing great! Just don't make a single mistake, or else you'll screw them up permanently and they might put you in a bad nursing home one day.

Love them through it all.

See? I told you raising teenagers is easy!

8. WHAT IS A GOOD MOM ANYWAY?

There was a time I tried hard, exceptionally hard, to be a 'good' mom.

I signed my kids up for all the right things and baked cookies and dressed them up in cute clothes. I taught them to read and put them on all the right teams and had playdates with all the people. I cooked nutritious meals and limited screen time and helped in their classrooms.

And while all those things were so worth doing, it's not what made me a good mom. It certainly didn't stop my kids from experiencing challenges or making some bad choices.

As we move into the teen years, I'm not even sure what a good mom looks like.

Is it holding your teenager's hand while she deals with crushing anxiety?

Is it keeping your temper in check when they look into your eyes and lie?

Is it pushing them to meet their potential or letting them fall on their face?

Is it letting them get behind the wheel again after having an accident that was their fault?

Can a good mom have a kid who gets bad grades, vapes, or sneaks out of their house?

Does a good mom let their kid on social media or do they monitor their every move?

Did a good mom ever have a child who cheated or stole or broke the law?

There was a time when I strived to be a good mom. There was a time I probably tried too hard.

But what I realized about these teenage years is we can only do what we think is right when raising our kids, and then the rest is up to luck and your child's choices.

Will an impulsive young teen join his friends who are throwing eggs at cars parked in their driveways?

Will an insecure girl decide not to get in an automobile with someone who has been drinking?

Will a shy adolescent say no to someone pushing them sexually or to drink or try drugs?

Will an impressionable 16-year-old remember safety protocols when someone tempts him online?

These are just a few of the tough choices our kids face, the ones raised by parents just doing their best. Good moms. Good dads.

So, I stopped trying to be a GOOD parent.

I just try to be THEIR parent, the one they need me to be at any given moment in their turbulent lives.

Sometimes I'm the parent who has strict rules and boundaries.

Sometimes I'm the one who picks up their room.

Sometimes I'm the one who may snoop on their phone when I fear something is wrong.

Sometimes I'm the one who stays up late helping them finish a project.

Sometimes I'm the one who won't drop off their forgotten assignment at school.

And sometimes, almost always, I'm still the one who bakes cookies. Or at least buys them at the store.

What I've learned from parenting teenagers is there are no 'good' parents, and there are no 'good' kids.

We're all just doing the best we can with the hand we got dealt.

And while we can try to play the odds and be smart and guess what might be coming next, a lot of it comes down to luck to see how our teens will play their cards.

We do our best to prepare them for the world in front of them, but their successes do not mean we are all good, and their failures do not mean we are all bad.

We make the best decisions we can for the kid who is in front of us, and we hope for the best.

I no longer want to be a good parent, whatever that means.

I want to be the parent my kids need, and however that looks on any given day – I'm okay with that.

9. It's Lonely Raising Teens

I've always heard about the loneliness when raising teens.

Most days, I don't understand it.

I don't understand it because my life with teenagers seems so full, so loud, so in-my-face 24 hours a day.

My schedule is packed with sports meets and dress shopping and book ordering. I constantly shuttle long, gangly bodies across town while stopping at the grocery store every day. Someone always wants me to write them a check or texts me to pick them up or yells down the stairs to say we are going to be late.

But in those moments when I'm in the thick of it, in those times when one of my children is talking back, is acting like the world ended, is lying to my face, the truth is, I've never felt so alone.

Because no one wants to highlight their kids' screw-ups on social media. No one wants to admit that you may have messed up this parenting gig. No one wants to make their teen a target or have them judged.

So, you wonder, "Why is my kid treating me like this?"

You ask yourself, "I don't see any other kids acting this way?"

You worry, "What kind of person am I raising?"

You feel alone in murky, shark-infested, unchartered waters, drowning in a sea of teenage angst.

You want to know more about the details of your teen's life, yet it often seems like you are watching a television show on mute. They decide what information to share and when to provide it to you, if at all.

And it is painful to know that your child is carrying around a heavy weight and knowing you are helpless to fix it.

When my kids were younger, I could strike up a conversation with another mother at a playground or a friend at a school event. I could easily share my parenting dilemmas and almost always find someone who could relate, which meant it was something I could fix.

But now, the problems are distinct, personal and sometimes taboo. They are issues I don't want to be shared and don't need additional judgment.

I start to crave time with my friends, people who love my kids like their own, yet it seems impossible to meet with them.

Whereas you once caught up at playdates and birthday parties or the occasional mom's night out starting at 7:30 when all of your kids were in bed, your life is now constantly apologizing for not being able to get together because of football games or band competitions or debate tournaments or college trips.

The irony is the heavier stuff we are dealing with requires trust, privacy, and connection, yet it's so hard to make that happen.

But most of all, I miss my kids before they are even gone, knowing that they are breaking free a little more every day.

They are the work of my past, but they have their own future. The end of their childhood is now closer than the beginning. And even in the midst of their breakdowns and snarkiness and eye-rolls, even when I wonder if I screwed this entire parenting job up, I know I will miss these glorious, sarcastic, messy, magnificent creatures. Every part of them.

The loneliness of raising teenagers is constant, palpable, perhaps even unavoidable.

And maybe even necessary to prepare us for what's coming next.

10. SOFT

I was reading a pretty hot debate in the comments section of a parenting group last night. A mom was complaining about the way her daughter was treating her, basically that sometimes the way the 15-year-old spoke to her was just mean and disrespectful.

There were two schools of thought on why kids today act out more. One was that the daughter had a 'safe space' to let out her emotions of the day, and while it was wrong, it was because she felt comfortable enough to do it. I agree with this concept as long as we don't become anyone's doormat.

The second theory was that parents today are just 'too soft', and we're raising a bunch of entitled brats who just want everything handed to them. Knowing so many wonderful teens and their parents, this theory makes me hot, particularly in today's chaotic modern world.

The common thread, however, is that almost everyone agreed that they would never have spoken to their parents that way. And truth be told, neither would I.

My parents would have knocked me into next Sunday if I had said a few of the things my kids said to me in the past. My mom and dad were so supportive, so loving, so empowering, but I also had a healthy dose of fear for them.

And the consequence of that fear was I didn't open up to them that much about the hard stuff, I never truly felt like I could come to them until I was much older.

I know many people who call me 'soft'. Most of the time it rolls right off me, but I felt a little defensive last night. I couldn't shake the feeling that my 'being soft' was a bad thing, but I was unsure how to put it into words.

A few weeks back, out of the blue at my dinner table, my daughter asked me if I was ever scared in college about getting roofied. "When did that start, Mom?" she asked.

And then my three daughters peppered me with questions. We had a long talk about frat parties and watching some of my friends drink too much. I shared a troubling encounter with a date that left me unnerved for months. I took a deep breath and told my three beautiful girls about a scary experience I had with drugs during my sophomore year of college.

They continued to ask, and I continued to answer, just as I have always done.

And that night I laid in my bed thankful that my daughters were comfortable enough with me to ask questions, comfortable enough with me to share some of their own experiences.

Yes, I haven't always liked the way my daughters have talked to me in the past. There have been times they were disrespectful or snotty or just cruel, times that words came out of their mouths that I never would have said to my parents.

But I also would never go to my parents to talk about drugs or alcohol. I would never go to my parents to talk about sex or my fears or problems.

I would never go to them to talk about anything difficult or uncomfortable.

They were great parents, and I respected them, but with that fear came an unspoken level of distrust that I couldn't open up to them.

Looking back at the last five years of parenting, I don't always like the way my teens have treated me, but I also know there have been a lot of times my kids have trusted me to be a place they could turn when they were unsure about this world.

Becoming a 'safe space' for your teens is a little bit of a tradeoff. You have to take the good with the bad, lose a little bit of power, believe that not responding to every behavior will make your relationship stronger instead of your role as a parent weaker.

You have to learn to disengage to keep them engaged. Say things like, "I know you're upset, but you can't talk to me that way. I'll be in my room if you'd like to discuss it," and then withhold the lecture.

Or sometimes just walk away saying something like, "I gave you an answer, and you know the consequences."

You have to set boundaries but be willing to move them. Rules, but be willing to change them depending on the circumstance. Grace, so much grace, for the unknown issues our teens face today.

And sometimes it means letting them lash out and being aware enough to know it's not about you – and hoping that one day they'll let you in to help them through whatever they are going through at the time.

So, yes, I'm soft, and I'm raising soft kids.

I'm soft because I try to be more flexible in this complex world. I'm soft because I believe my kids are getting pushed and pressured from all directions, much more than I did growing up. I'm soft so my kids know they can come to me about anything and get honest answers about tough issues.

Soft has made our relationship strong. Soft has made them self-confident. Soft has made them feel safe.

And if loving hard makes me soft, I'm okay with that.

11. I WISH SOMEONE HAD TOLD ME

I wish someone would have told me what raising a teenager was like.

I wish someone told me there would be days my heart would break in half for them, that my soul would be crushed by the weight of their sorrow.

I wish someone told me that I would experience doubt at every parenting decision, confusion over choices, fear at every juncture.

I wish someone told me about the extreme highs they experience because of victories and achievements and simple pleasures, and also the extreme lows that come on like a slingshot in the opposite direction.

I wish someone would have told me how deeply teenagers feel, and that sometimes it can be terrifying to watch, so much so that you sleep next to them like you did when they were small just to get to the next sunrise.

I wish someone told me that there would be times when you didn't like your child, when you wondered where you went wrong, when you sat up late into the night worrying about who they may become.

I wish someone told me the passion they can feel for their interests, their friendships, their life and how important it is to help them find healthy pursuits, so they don't fill their time with drama or mindless tasks.

I didn't know it would be this hard.

I wish someone told me that staying close means letting go and that teenagers need so much space to grow.

I wish someone told me how very smart, very funny, very enjoyable they can be – when they are in the mood and the stars are aligned.

I wish someone told me how forgiving they are when their parents make mistakes, how compassionate they are when you give them a chance.

I wish someone told me how much hope these teens would give me in the darkest of times.

I wish someone told me that despite their behavior and attitude, teenagers need structure and rules and discipline – they even want it so they know where they stand in this crazy world.

I wish someone told me that nobody knows what they are doing when parenting a teenager.

I wish someone told me how lonely it felt when facing problems with your teenager, how hard it is to respect their privacy, how their stories are not yours to tell.

I wish someone told me that watching your teenagers chase – and if lucky – achieve their goals and dreams would be infinitely better than achieving yours.

I wish someone told me that you will get through the challenging times, and your relationship will be stronger because of it.

I wish someone told me how much they eat, how much they sleep, how much they want to be driven to places at all hours of the day and night.

I wish someone told me how they will listen to other people more than their parents – and how hard it is not to say I told you so. I wish someone told me how hard it would be to bite my tongue at every juncture and not lecture at every opportunity.

I wish someone told me the importance of choosing your battles – and that some battles aren't worth fighting for.

I wish someone would have told me how much I would laugh and how much I would dance, how many videos I would watch and shoes I would buy, how I would go without sleep to pick them up and get up early to get a goodbye kiss, how I would suddenly look up into their eyes and they would be the one to comfort me, instead of the other way around.

I wish someone would have told me what parenting a teenager would be like, but I probably wouldn't have believed a word they said.

It's so much harder, so much better, so much more beautiful and terrifying and love-filled than anything anyone could describe.

And I wouldn't change a thing

12. THEY WILL SAY NO

They will say no most of the time.

When you ask them to watch a movie on a Friday night.

Or go for a walk after dinner.

Or search for sand crabs on a warm summer evening on a beach vacation.

But sometimes, if you are lucky, you get a yes.

It might be begrudgingly or with a small dose of smug attitude. It may be because of some guilt you dropped or a promise to let them do something else the next evening of their choosing. It may even be the result of a little threat from Dad.

But sometimes, if you are lucky, you get a yes from your big kid to do something together, and for a brief moment, time stands still, like a portrait an artist doesn't want to finish because he doesn't want to give it to someone else.

And at the moment after they say yes, you may hear the giggle you fell in love with so many years ago when playing Legos or hosting tea parties or letting her walk around in your favorite heels.

Or you feel the familiar warmth of a hand, now larger than yours, that rests comfortably in your palm from years of walking through parking lots or crossing busy streets.

Or you see a smile cross your daughter's face, one you've seen a million times when you used to walk into a room, and you are so grateful for just one more appearance.

In these challenging teenage years, they will say no most of the time, because that is what they are supposed to do.

In saying no – to be with their friends, to forge new paths, to figure out who they are meant to be – they prepare themselves for their future, and they prepare us for our new world as well. A world where we are no longer the center of their universe.

But sometimes, when we are lucky, we get a yes. And it's up to us to make the most of it.

There is still so much magic to be had with our big kids, with our growing kids, with our kids who are no longer kids.

And I plan on taking advantage of every yes because I always want them to know I'll never stop asking for just one more moment with them.

13. Sometimes Good Kids Make Bad Decisions

There's a reason why parents of big kids shut down when their kids hit the teenage years.

There's a reason why moms stop talking to other parents at school pick-up lines and dads avoid people at all cost.

You know that phrase, 'Little kids, little problems. Big kids, bigger problems?' It is so true.

And if you are lucky enough to raise a teenager that never drank or smoked or did drugs, if you are lucky enough to have a child that never got arrested for a misdemeanor or snuck out or cheated on a test, if you are lucky enough never to feel like you were just a complete and utter failure as a parent because of the behavior of your kid despite your best efforts, consider it just that: *lucky*.

Because for most big kids who do something bad, it is usually not from bad parenting as much as the teen making a bad decision in the heat of the moment.

And we need to sit on that for a second.

Before we rush to judgment. Before we roll our eyes and start mentioning all the things we think those parents did wrong. Before we fill ourselves with righteous indignation.

We need to remember that it could be our kid, and how we want people to treat us.

Sure, we need to be conscientious parents and raise our kids to the best of our abilities. But unless you have severely neglected, abused, or traumatized your child, we need to recognize that sometimes teenagers lose their way despite our best efforts.

Addiction can be genetic. Violence could be linked to a traumatic event not related to the parents. Stealing could be attention-seeking behavior. Lying is testing boundaries. Mental health is determined by so many internal and external factors.

But also, teenagers are poor decision-makers if they feel pressured, stressed or want attention from peers, so while with one friend, a teen may say no to alcohol, at a party with peers they want to impress, they may engage in binge drinking in a spur-of-the-moment request.

Rather than blaming the parents, we need to rally around families who need support instead of pushing them further underwater.

I still believe as parents we are the number one role models for our kids. I still believe that we can arm our children with information and boundaries so they grow up into productive adults. I still believe we can teach our kids right from wrong.

But I also believe that most of us are trying our best and parent with the best of intentions.

I speak from experience. Sometimes good kids just make bad decisions. Sometimes good kids have addictions. Sometimes good kids are hurting and don't know how to express it. Sometimes good kids cave under pressure. Sometimes good kids want to impress their peers so they do something bad.

And oftentimes, these good kids come from good parents.

There is enough guilt when it comes to parenting. Did I do too much for them? Not enough? Did I give them too much freedom? Was I too overbearing? Many parents spend the rest of their lives wondering where they went wrong when raising their kids.

So, the next time your local rumor mill starts running with the bad behavior of a child coming from a 'good' family, maybe resist the urge to spread the gossip to another friend.

Instead, maybe use it as a discussion springboard with your own child.

And if you are feeling extra generous, reach out to that parent who is most likely beating themselves up for their child's behavior, the one who feels isolated, the one who is staying up all night examining every parenting decision she ever made.

They could use some support, too.

You get to choose.

14. They Say Sleep When the Baby Sleeps

When your kids are little, they say to sleep when your baby sleeps.

When your kid turns into a teenager, you don't ever sleep because:

They are out in someone else's car, and you just pray they are responsible and safe;

They need to be somewhere at the crack of dawn, so you're up to make sure they get there on time;

You're waiting for them to pull into the driveway after being out with friends, and you can't fall asleep until they walk through your door;

You want to see how their night at work went;

They are out at a dance or a sporting event or a school trip or an activity, and you sit and wonder if they are okay and know how much they are loved;

They are stressed about school, so you are too;

They received their first broken heart, so yours broke too.

They are just a few feet from you down the hall, in their room,

with the door closed--and you wonder what is going on in

that head, so you stay awake wondering if they are okay.

And sometimes, just as you are about to close your eyes for the night at 11 p.m., your teen comes running into your room and plops into your bed giggling like when she was five years old–and even though you are so exhausted from the day, you lay with her for just a little bit longer.

You listen to her talk about some YouTuber you've never heard of and Harry Styles' new album and the boy who cracks jokes in her social studies class and the test she has coming up in chemistry and how she wants to go to the mall on Saturday.

At that moment, you wouldn't trade any amount of sleep for that time. You would stay awake all night to feel that closeness. You will take the exhaustion that comes in the morning and hits you like a ton of bricks because those few minutes were the best part of your day.

So, my best advice to new parents. Sleep when the baby sleeps.

Because you're going to be awake a lot during the teenage years too, and you're not going to want to miss a minute.

15. Raising Teens Can Feel One-Sided

Someone once told me, "When you can't have the relationship you want with your child, you focus on giving them the relationship you think they need."

I didn't understand that at the time.

I mean, a relationship takes two. It should be based on honesty and mutual respect and understanding. That was the type of relationship I wanted with my kids. That was the relationship I expected.

I wanted them to come to me with all their problems. I wanted to have an open and honest relationship. I wanted them to know they could come to me for anything.

And then I had teenagers.

The truth is, I do have this relationship with my three teens... sometimes.

There are times they have come to me when they are in trouble or need advice. And sometimes, they have hidden things from me or sneaked around or acted belligerent.

There are times we have deep, meaningful discussions, and there are times they shut me out with a force that takes my breath away.

There are times our house is peaceful and enjoyable, and times they are so argumentative I want to throw a tantrum of my own.

And honestly, there are times my relationship with them is not what I hoped it to be. Not even close.

So, I give them the relationship I think they need instead of getting upset about the relationship I want to have with them.

This means I set boundaries, both on what they are allowed to do and how they treat me. I share these with my kids so they know I have a healthy respect for myself and how I should be treated. I set boundaries to keep them safe.

I give space and grace whenever I can. This may mean giving up on a family dinner for a few nights or ignoring the snarky remark or even enduring a few painful days where I wonder what is going on behind that closed bedroom door.

And I work on myself, which is really the only thing I can control. I focus on gratitude and start my day by reminding myself of the qualities I love about my kids. It's easy to fall into a spiral of expecting the worst about our teens and then only seeing those things.

I do something for them, like folding their laundry or making their favorite meal. I want them to know that even when things aren't right between us, I'm still there for them.

I send them a text or a funny meme I saw to try and keep the communication lines open. I don't expect a response.

And I wait for them to come back to me.

Sometimes we go into these teen years expecting a certain type of relationship and spend this time trying to force it into happening. We have a constant power struggle with our child, a draining tug of war without a winner.

We can fight with them every step of the way, or we can try to give them the relationship they need during this time.

It doesn't mean they get to do whatever they want, but it means surrendering the idea of how you thought your relationship would be with them – which is harder than it sounds.

The definition of insanity is doing the same thing over and over again and expecting a different result. That's why the teen years are so hard.

You feel crazy during this challenging time because we try to have a solid relationship with them, but it doesn't always work the way we want.

So we have to try something different. When you can't change their behavior, you have to try and change yours.

Give them the relationship they need, and then work on yourself too.

I'm not saying it's easy. But I am saying they're worth it.

16. We Do What We Can

We will never know if we are doing it right with our big kids.

We will never know if we said the right words.

We will never know if we gave them too much, or maybe not enough.

We will question all our decisions. We will regret things we said. We will beat ourselves up and worry and wonder.

But this right here.

This is what we can always get right.

When things don't go their way. When life pushes them down. When their hearts are broken, and they feel unworthy, and their spirit is crushed to the core.

We can envelop them in love when they need it the most. We can erase some of their grief with our strong embrace. We can make them feel safe and remind them that they have a place in this world, no matter what happens.

Our big kids, they still need us.

We can't fix their problems like we used to, but we can do one better.

We can love them through it all – the glory, the celebrations, the failures, the sadness.

We can be their soft place to land in a challenging world.

We can wrap our arms around them or talk them through a problem or show up when they need us most – and let them know tomorrow is another day.

Our big kids, they still need us.

And while every parent wants to take their child's pain away, we can do something even more powerful.

We can help them get through trying times — and let them know they are strong enough to get to the other side.

And while I'll never enjoy watching my kids hurt, knowing we can still ease their pain, well, that's a little sweet, too.

17. LET HER BECOME

They say the most important thing you can do as a parent is let your child become who they want to be.

For years she wore the clothes I wanted, did the activities I signed her up for, and people-pleased the heck out of me.

And truth be told, she made it simple for us to get along. She was an easy kid.

But in the last year, she is finding her voice, her style, her beliefs. She is formulating her own opinions and choices and dreams.

And it is hard. And it is beautiful. And it is challenging.

We don't see eye to eye on most things, and our relationship is more work. Sometimes it's exhausting, sometimes it's full of tears, sometimes I am so exasperated I want to throw in the towel.

But I can also see the promise of greatness in her dreams.

I see her strength in her convictions.

I see the kindness in her eyes.

And our love and bond hold strong.

I recognize that an easier relationship with me doesn't necessarily translate to a more productive adult.

I have to be okay with that.

So, while sometimes I wonder where that little girl went who thought I hung the moon, I am also loving this challenging woman emerging in front of me – the one who is changing me a little bit, too.

And while I may not support all her choices, I know that letting her make as many as possible will be the glue that keeps our relationship intact.

So, I let go to hold on, and watch as she starts to take flight.

It may not be the route I would have suggested, but I take comfort in knowing I taught her to fly.

18. You Take What You Can Get

You take what you can get when raising teenagers.

You hold onto the beautiful moments. And there will be beautiful moments.

But those beautiful moments will rarely be when you expect it, and definitely not when you try to create them.

It won't be when they stay up late and you want them to get up early, all perky and ready to go pick out a Christmas tree. They may sulk in the back seat and grunt one-word answers to important questions like, "Do you like it or do you love it? Is this tree as big as last year? Who is ready to decorate?"

It won't be right after an exhausting day at school and sports practice when they dread facing a pile of homework even though you have barely seen them and crave their needing you.

It won't be when even though you cooked their favorite meal or bought them those new shoes or let them take that trip with their friends – they still seem unhappy, unsatisfied, undone.

And you'll rarely know why they lash out at times when you so desperately want them to feel loved. I often think they have no idea either.

The beautiful moments come when you are least ready for them.

When you're sitting in a fast-food booth sharing milkshakes, and your daughter asks your advice about how to talk to a boy she likes.

When you go into their room late one evening to say good night and you end up talking for an hour. And you don't care that you are missing out on much-needed sleep.

When you are standing in the kitchen washing dishes and two long, gangly arms wrap themselves around your body and squeeze so tightly that your heart feels like it may burst.

When they say, "Mom, let's take a selfie to remember this day." And you didn't even realize how special the day was to them.

Don't believe the myth that teens are always miserable and moody and salty and snarky.

I mean, they totally can be all of these things, and it's often with their parents, but it's not all of the time.

There are beautiful moments left to be had raising teenagers, if you are patient enough to wait for them.

But you need to step back and not force it. These beautiful moments will often be on their terms, and that's okay, too.

If you let them, these amazing young people will surprise you by opening their hearts so wide and loving so fiercely and confounding expectations so much that it will knock your socks off – and it will be beautiful.

I promise you, it's worth it.

19. She Doesn't Know

Right now, she doesn't care about the nights I lie awake worrying about her future.

She doesn't care about the tears I shed after our last fight.

She doesn't care that we agonized over decisions and stressed about choices and sometimes struggled with what to do next.

Right now, she doesn't remember when I was her whole world, when she begged me to lay down with her, when my hugs could make everything better.

She doesn't remember following me everywhere and grabbing onto my leg whenever she needed to steady herself.

She doesn't remember falling asleep in my arms.

Right now, she's busy trying to find herself, find her voice, find her place in this world.

She's busy with her peers, school, and all the things on her phone.

She's busy trying to break free from the ties that bind us, she's trying to emerge into her own light.

And while she's busy doing all the things, while we're on this roller coaster ride together, I dig deep and remain thankful for the little things.

Like 5:30 a.m. wake-up calls when I get to see her do what she loves. And text messages with a million emojis thanking me for washing her uniform. And conversations that happen way past my bedtime, but when she shares what happened during her big night out.

I'm thankful for the smile I see when she does well on a test. I'm grateful for the cool summer nights that let us spend a few extra minutes on our patio. I'm happy she'll still let me hug her before she goes to bed.

And the rest of the time, she spends it trying to break free.

But there's something that daughters don't know until much later in life.

More often than not, daughters come back to their mothers, even after breaking away.

They remember those nights they cried in our arms. They care about the memories of baking cookies and playing in sprinklers and eating ice cream on Friday nights. They find time to call their mothers and go shopping and sit to have tea. They remember the little things.

I know this, because I was a teen daughter once too.

And despite the way I treated my mom in my teens, despite my 'pushing her away' and 'fighting her affections' and 'believing she was holding me back', she patiently waited for me to come back to her – just as I will be waiting for my daughters, too.

So I stay connected to her in whatever small ways I can, grateful for whatever time she'll give me.

And when she's ready, I will be waiting with open arms.

Because that's what mothers do for their daughters who spend their teen years breaking free

20. HAVE I LOVED HER ENOUGH?

Have I loved her enough?

Have I built up her self-esteem so she can handle whatever the world throws at her today?

Does she know that she has value? Does she recognize her potential? Does she understand that she is worthy – of respect, consideration, and love?

Did I do enough to make her feel confident to say no to the wrong things, but more importantly, yes to the right ones?

Did I spend enough time teaching her to be kind and inclusive? Did I spend enough time teaching her what to do when people are not kind and inclusive?

Will she remember what's important when the time comes to choose? Will she remember she can come to me when she makes a mistake?

Did I teach her how to stand up for herself? Did I teach her how to be assertive? Did I teach her not to give up on her dreams?

Have I loved her enough?

These are the thoughts that swirl around my mind each and every time I watch her walk outside of our home and into the chaotic world beyond my control.

Time is moving so quickly lately that sometimes it takes my breath away. There are so many things I want to tell her, so many things left to do.

But her life is so full of school and sports and activities, so full of friendships and TikToks and selfies, so full of learning and doing and growing.

So full of getting to ready to fly to her next chapter.

And I wonder, have I loved her enough?

Each time she leaves, my heart trails behind her, like one of those clipped tags on her gigantic backpack. Her steps are confident, and her head is held high.

Sometimes, right before she leaves, she turns around and flashes that beautiful smile that makes my heart skip a beat every time.

And I'll always question if I've loved her enough to face this world, but I know I've loved her as much as any mother can.

21. PORCH LIGHT

I've been leaving our porch light on a lot recently. My teenagers arrive late in the evening, from sports and activities, from dates and parties, from work and babysitting – and I want them to see their way back into our home.

So, I leave the porch light on.

And I think, as parents, that's all we can do as our kids start to leave our haven for a little bit longer each time – let them know they have an entryway back to their safe place.

So, I leave the porch light on. I keep the refrigerator full of snacks. I leave my bedroom door open when they are home. I offer rides when I know they can drive themselves. I make their favorite meals.

I do these things now so they know they can always come home, so they want to come home, so they know they can always turn to me in the good and the bad.

It's a rough ride raising teenagers, and sometimes I understand why birds push their babies out of the nest. The tug-of-war between their desire for independence and their parents' need for boundaries to keep them safe can simply be exhausting.

But no matter how trying a time it is, no matter how many growing pains we experience, no matter how much we butt heads, I want them to know they can always come home.

I'll make sure the porch light is always on for them in whatever way I can.

22. The Circle of a Mother's Love

Let me tell you a little story about the circle of life and the circle of a mother's love.

Yesterday, my 80-year-old mom told my nearly 50-year-old self to bring my laundry upstairs. Then, she instructed me on how to clean a pot I've had for two decades. And then, when I was packing a few boxes for returns, she reminded me to make sure I blacked out the labels or else the post office wouldn't know what to scan.

And that's when I responded with, "Mom! This isn't the first time I've done this, you know!"

She just laughed at me and drank her tea and rearranged her magic purse that has everything in it – from medicine for every ailment and tissues to nail clippers and candy.

I don't know why I responded so curtly. I guess I just was tired and didn't want to be told what to do.

The irony wasn't lost on me when throughout the day, I said things to my teenagers like, "Hey, did you send in that form yet?" and, "Take your coat upstairs," and, "OMG! Put that bowl in the dishwasher."

And each time, they responded with the obligatory, "I know, Mom!"

I would laugh at their exasperation and return to what I was doing.

Last night, my 16-year-old and I went to the wake of a lovely woman who happened to be the grandmother of my daughter's best friend.

As I hugged my friend, the mom to my daughter's bestie and the daughter of the deceased, I watched as one of her kids brought a pair of tweezers back to her.

She explained, "As we were coming here, I just started throwing everything in my purse that I thought I would need, just in case. Of course, one of the kids needed these. My mom always did that for us."

And I couldn't help but think about grandmas and their special purses, and how mothers show their love.

Sometimes we show it by nagging – or gently reminding – about looming deadlines and chores that need to be done.

Sometimes it's by setting rules and boundaries to keep them safe.

Sometimes it's by doing laundry when your child – no matter what their age – doesn't have the time or cooking a special meal or changing sheets.

Sometimes it's laughing off a snarky comment.

And sometimes, it's simply being there, saying nothing at all.

The universe showed me something pretty special yesterday.

It reminded me of all the love I give and receive throughout the small details of my life, and how lucky I am to have it spread through three generations right now.

A mother's love is rarely shown in grand gestures, but if we're lucky, it's woven into a lifetime of small, meaningful moments of kindness and selflessness and generosity that knows no bounds.

And when the time comes, in the magic purses grandmothers carry – when these grand women start slowing down but still want to be there for their family.

Until it's time to pass that tradition on to the mothers coming after. Forever and ever. Again and again.

Love your people hard today, in whatever small ways you can show it. Treasure the ways they show their love to you. Don't take one second for granted.

SECTION 2:

DEAR TEENS, THIS IS WHAT I WANT YOU TO KNOW

INTRODUCTION

I try to never tell parents of young kids that it goes by so fast. Or, enjoy every second because, wait until the teenage years.

I try, with all my heart, to be encouraging instead of using platitudes.

But what I will tell other parents is when it comes to the teenage years, it's not that time speeds up, but the amount of time you get to spend with them goes down significantly.

And even though my three teen daughters either look me in the eyes (or down to me from their five-foot-ten frame), there is so much I want them to know.

About loving themselves and loving someone else.

About friendship.

About taking care of their mental health and finding joy.

About empowering others and empowering themselves.

And even a little bit about why I parent the way I do.

Sometimes, and maybe I'm wrong on this, but sometimes it seems like they are not listening to me.

So, I sometimes I would write to them in letter form and share those letters with other parents. I started to jot down messages I wanted them to know and memories I didn't want to forget. I wrote about specific periods of time, what stood out to me during them.

I am so touched when I see parents tagging their kids or telling me they emailed my piece to their son or daughter. I get chills when someone says they read it aloud to their teen. I might even get a little teary when someone says it's exactly what they want their child to know but couldn't put into words.

On the pages that follow are my favorite letters and captured moments.

I hope that you can take a sliver of my heart and apply it to your own unique situation – and if you want to share it with your teenager, even better.

I'm not saying they won't roll their eyes, but if it gives you an opportunity to open a connection with them? Well, that's everything to me.

23. SORRY, NOT SORRY

Dear teenagers of mine:

I'm sorry that you got 'that' mom.

I'm sorry you got that mom who will always ask where you are going – and actually expect you to be there.

I'm sorry that you got the mom who wants to meet the parents of the house you want to go to, or the boy you want to date, or the friend you want to spend time with after school.

I'm sorry that you got the mom who checks your screen time and your social media and your entire phone every once in a while.

I'm sorry you got that mom who expects you to carry your weight around the house, who thinks doing things like emptying the dishwasher and washing your own clothes and making your bed are important life skills.

I'm sorry you got that mom that lets you fail sometimes. I'm sorry that I don't always bring the gym uniform you left sitting on the counter or your homework sitting on your desk to school. It hurts my heart when something bad happens to you, but I hope the consequences teach you more.

I'm sorry that you got that mom who says 'no' when all the rest of the moms are saying 'yes'. I know that sucks for you. It sucks for me too. Sometimes other parents don't like it when I'm 'that' mom, either.

It's a delicate balancing act, raising you. I want you to be independent, yet one mistake can change the trajectory of your young life. I want you to be accepted by your peers, but not at the expense of risking safety. I want you to become trustworthy, but sometimes I know – or you've demonstrated – you can't yet be trusted.

So, I'm 'that' mom. Just like my mom was 'that' mom, too.

And I hope that one day you'll understand. I hope one day you'll appreciate the fact that holding you accountable, setting limits, letting you learn from your mistakes – being 'that' mom – is the greatest way I can show my love for you.

But until that time, I'm (kind of) sorry that you got stuck with me. I know that it makes you embarrassed, I know that it takes away some of your fun, I know that it sometimes makes your relationships contentious or difficult.

So, I'll say yes when I can, when it comes to your style or your activities or what you want to get out of your future.

I want you to be happy and enjoy life. It's nice when you fit in. And sometimes I don't want a knock-down, drag-out fight about every 'ask' either.

But there are times when saying no is important, even when – especially when – every other parent is saying yes.

Unfortunately for you though, I'm going to keep being 'that' mom, and that's just the way it's going to be.

24. IF YOU PUT YOURSELF OUT THERE

D ear daughters,
    If you put yourself out there into the world, some people aren't going to like you.

If you say what you feel, push back, go against the norm, some people are going to ostracize you.

Even if you try to do everything right, even if you kill with kindness, even if you think you are showing the world your best self, you will get unfriended and talked about and ignored.

But my dearest daughters, if you put yourself out there, you will (eventually) find your people, and they will love you fiercely for all that you are.

If you stand up for what you believe in, you will build connections that last a lifetime.

If you try to do what you think is right, you will make mistakes, but you'll be able to look at yourself in the mirror and do better tomorrow.

Don't defer your wants and needs so much that you deny yourself simple pleasures – so you understand what makes you happy.

Don't pursue activities because you think it will make your parents, your friends or anyone else like you – because you may miss out on your true calling.

Don't try to fix every situation, every problem, every broken person, because it's not your job or responsibility – and you need to learn to develop healthy give-and-take relationships. It's okay to say no, and it's okay to not chase after someone who has walked through the exit sign of your life.

Don't see your self-worth from the perceived opinions of others.

Don't be afraid of letting anyone else down – feel the fear and use it to fuel the discovery of finding your place.

And give the best of yourself to this world.

Because you won't get, nor do you need the approval of others.

Dear daughters, put yourself out into this world with everything that you are.

Find joy in yourself, and you won't need anyone to give it to you.

And that's what life is all about.

25. BE THE GIRL

Dear daughters,
   Be 'that' girl.

Be the girl who reaches behind and pulls the next person up to where you are in life. Do this because you know that success isn't finite and there's enough room at the top for everyone.

Be the girl who waits at the finish line until the rest of the team crosses. Recognize their effort, not what place they earned. People will always remember how you made them feel, not where you finished.

Be the first to congratulate someone when they get what you want. Try to be happy for them even when your heart is breaking.

Be the girl who gently tells another woman that she has food in her teeth or a tag on her shirt or toilet paper on her shoe. Mocking someone else's misfortune isn't cool.

Be the girl who has a firm handshake and looks people in the eye. Remember that a simple 'hello' and smile can change someone's day.

Be the girl who doesn't seek approval from others. It never feels as good as when you are happy with yourself.

Be the girl who knows that not everyone will like her, no matter how hard you try. You can be the best tea in the cupboard, but some people will never pick you because they just don't like tea.

Be the girl who sets goals and works hard to achieve them. Encourage your friends to chase their dreams, too, and then support each other every step of the way.

Be the girl who tells another girl that there's always room for one more. Remember that life is not an exclusive club.

Be the girl who says 'no': no to dangerous situations, to doing things before you are ready, to decisions that you can't take back. You shouldn't have to put yourself in jeopardy to get someone else to like you.

Be the girl who loves herself, because what's not to love?

Dear daughter, be the girl, become the woman you were born to be.

Because for you, sweet girl, the only thing we truly want you to be is happy and loved. The rest is the cherry already on top of a perfect sundae.

26. When the World Tells You that You Aren't Enough

Dear Daughter,

I saw your smiling face crumble out of the corner of my eye. I noticed you stopped scrolling on your phone and looked deeper into the screen. Your body that was sitting comfortably in our minivan went rigid, and then you shifted in the leather seat to look out the window towards snowy trees and empty soccer fields.

Your sigh sounded like you had the entire world on your shoulders. When we stopped at a traffic light, I turned and softly asked,

"Are you okay, honey? Is something wrong?"

And you replied, "No, Mom. Everything's cool."

But I knew it wasn't. Someone in this world just told you that you weren't enough.

I knew better than to pry. I've learned the hard way when dealing with teenagers that fewer questions usually lead to more answers – eventually.

That knowledge didn't stop me from wanting to take you in my arms and protect your beautiful spirit or wonder what it was that changed your mood.

There are so many times this world will try to beat you down, so many times people will tell you that you are not worthy.

Was it your grades? Please know your GPA, your class rank, or what college you attend can't measure your goodness.

Remember that life is about the impact you have on others, so work on building your brain and growing your heart, and the rest will fall into place.

Was it a picture you saw on Instagram or a mean-spirited message on Snapchat?

Please know that what others do on social media is not about you, sweet girl. Give that person the benefit of the doubt and try to give them grace.

What people write online says infinitely more about them than it will ever say about you.

Was it an ad you saw with a supermodel who sported perfect hair and a killer body? Did that make you feel disappointed in your appearance?

In this crazy world, the media tells women they are inadequate a minimum of one thousand times a day, and photo editing changes what we think is 'normal'.

You will want whiter teeth or straighter hair. Nicer clothes. Plumper lips and thinner thighs. I wish I could say it gets better, but it doesn't – it all depends on how you see yourself. Fight the urge to conform and love what makes you unique. Remember, cookie cutters should be used in baking and not for people.

Did someone break your trust? Unfortunately, this will happen a lot over the years. Your friends or people you date may not adhere to the same standard of privacy as you do, or their desire to feel 'in the know' is more important than your relationship. Learn that when people show you who they are, you need to believe them – but never forget that some friends also deserve a second chance.

Go with your gut.

Are you sad for someone else? I hope you never sit idly by when someone else gets treated poorly. You must live with yourself and adhere to your moral compass. Remember to use your voice. It is stronger than you think.

Dear daughter, I know you may never tell me what sunk your spirit today, I may never know who told you that you are not enough. But please remember this: no person or achievement, no amount of likes or fans, no number on the scale or score on a test can make you happy.

It is a choice you have to make every day, and it is hard. Find what makes you the happiest and do a lot of that.

And know that you are exactly enough as you are at this moment.

Anyone telling you differently just wants to feel enough too.

27. Don't Be a People Pleaser Like Me

Dear daughters: don't be like me.

Don't spend your youth trying to please everyone but yourself.

Don't spend your time always trying to do all the right things, to be the right person, so others will approve of you.

Don't be defined by what you think others want, what others expect, of you.

Don't get trapped in the role of living as a people pleaser.

Don't worry so much about trying to get someone to like you that you forget you are already likable.

Don't worry about earning anyone else's approval – not a teacher's, not a coach's, not a boy's or a friend's, not even your parents' – because you are already worthy.

I did all the right things for all the wrong reasons.

When I was your age, I worked hard to be the whole package. I wanted to get good grades because I thought getting into a good college would please my mom. I tried to be a leader at school because I knew it would make my dad proud. I became a cheerleader because I thought that would make me liked by others, and joined clubs only because of my friends.

And while I was happy and lived a great life, I felt unsatisfied because I never found out who I was, who I wanted to become, until much later in life.

Like most young girls, I wanted – I needed – to be liked, so I lived my life in a way to make that happen. And when someone didn't like me, when I didn't meet someone's expectations, I was crushed.

What I didn't realize: you can be the ripest, juiciest, most unblemished peach in the box, but some people just don't like peaches. It had nothing to do with me.

I want you to know that the only person whose approval you need is your own.

So, dear daughters, don't be like me.

Don't let your natural kindness inhibit you from saying 'no' to things you don't want to do – so you can find your passions instead.

Don't defer your wants and needs so much that you deny yourself simple pleasures – so you understand what makes you happy.

Don't pursue activities because you think it will make your parents, your friends or anyone else like you – because you may miss out on your true calling.

Don't try to fix every situation, every problem, every broken person, because it's not your job or responsibility – because you need to learn to develop healthy give-and-take relationships. It's OK to say no.

Don't see your self-worth from the perceived opinions of others.

Don't be afraid of letting anyone else down – feel the fear and use it to fuel the discovery of finding your place in this world.

You are already kind. You are already thoughtful. And you are already so loved.

Free yourself of the shackles of anyone else's expectations now, so you can find your best life earlier than your mom did.

Dear daughters, don't be like me.

Because it took me a long time, but I finally figured out that I deserved better than living for others' approval.

Living for my own is so much better.

28. TAKE YOUR JOY

Dear kids:
　　　There's something you need to know.

Happiness in this life isn't a given.

No matter how much money you have, no matter how fit you are, no matter how much someone else loves you, finding and keeping your happiness is a full-time job.

And you have to take charge of it. You have to own it.

No one can make you happy. No one can make you fulfilled or content. Not a partner, not a job, not money, and not even children you love more than life itself.

Happiness is a choice you have to make, and it is hard.

To be happy, you have to fight off feelings of guilt and inadequacy and the desire to please. You have to let go of the idea of perfection and see the beauty in the chaos of your life. You have to take responsibility – for your actions, for your words, for your mistakes. And you can't try to control everything either (trust me on this one), which only leads to disappointment.

Happiness won't just come to you. You have to reach out and take it. Even be a little greedy with it. You have to fill your life with things that bring YOU joy, and sometimes that means ignoring what others want you to do. It also means putting up some serious boundaries for those who want to bring their chaos into your world.

I know that it sounds easy in theory, but it is difficult for most women. It's been difficult for me.

You must strive for connection – to people, to passions, to art, to anything that brings you peace and contentment. You need to work hard to create deeper relationships with friends and family and find gratitude for the little things.

And when you find yourself yearning for peace, when you find yourself desperately wanting to fill a happiness void in your life, remember there is no tangible such as food, alcohol, drugs, shopping, etc., that will make you feel whole. These are short-term fixes and will never solve your problems.

You won't be happy every moment or even every day. And that's okay. We all face bad times.

But the important thing is when things look bleak, you know how to find joy, you know how to pull yourself out of the shadows, you know what to do to make sure you feel at peace with yourself.

And when you get lost in the darkness, you know to ask for help.

What is the best part of achieving happiness and contentment as a woman?

When you're happy, you want to lift others up as well. You can spread compliments and compassion and grace around like confetti – which makes everyone feel good.

Sometimes your happiness and your peace will mean cutting out the negativity in your life. This might mean less social media or saying 'no' to toxic people.

Do not believe it when someone says this is selfish. You must protect your happiness with every fiber of your being. Resentment and guilt are heavy burdens to offload in your life.

If you learn anything from me, sweet girls, I want you to see how I found my happiness and peace in this complicated life.

You bring me so much joy, but being happy? That comes from deep within myself, and it took me a long time to get here.

Find out what makes you the happiest, sweet kids, and then make the time to do it.

You deserve all the happiness you can get out of this life.

As do we all.

29. I Wear Your Pain

D ear child,
        I wear your pain.

The first time I heard your cry, I put your pain on like a cloak, ready to protect you from any darkness in this world, knowing I would never give up fighting for you.

I wear your pain.

I feel every blow, every bump, every bruise that happens to your body. When you're sick, the weight of your illness makes me feel soggy like a wet sweater; when you're injured, I hold you tight in hopes that your discomfort will transfer to me.

I wear your pain.

When you get left out, your hurt drapes over my mood, your disappointment lays sadly on my mind. My heart weighs heavy when the world rears its ugly head toward you on those days when you feel like you aren't enough.

Even when you don't tell me – especially when you don't tell me – I try to ease your burdens.

I wear your pain.

I grit my teeth when I watch you make mistakes, knowing you need to learn how to survive in this world. I fall to my knees and pray you stay safe, aware of the danger that lurks outside the walls of our home. I try to absorb your fears like water into a sponge so you face your life with courage and conviction.

And I ache when your heart aches, suffer when your soul suffers, and sometimes I cry, knowing that my hugs and kisses and chocolate chip cookies no longer dull your troubles or can mask your misery.

As you grow older, the weight sometimes gets heavier. I want to help you navigate these murky waters, but I know it's a journey you must take yourself.

So, I follow behind, waiting to help you pick up the pieces, cheering you on every step of the way.

I wear your pain, in the hopes you know you're not alone. I wear your pain to lessen the depth of your own, so you will always have the strength to rise back up again. I wear your pain, so you can lean into the dark places – and so you will know that I will always pull you back out.

I wear your pain with tenderness and sympathy and warmth.

I wear your pain, so you don't ever have to wear it like a scar, so you don't feel broken, so you never feel hopeless before the next dawn arrives.

I wear your pain, so you know that you are not your mistakes, you are not your past, you are not what took you down for a moment in time.

I wear your pain, dear child.

For as long as I have breath in my lungs and bones in my body and a heart that beats.

I wear your pain – simply because that's what parents do for their children, as you will do for yours one day, too.

30. Sometimes I Say the Wrong Thing

Dear teenager,

I know I give you a hard time about your room a lot. I know I get frustrated when you are on your phone. I know you feel overwhelmed with academics and service projects and sports.

And I keep saying the wrong thing at the wrong time.

Trust me, you aren't a peach, either.

We are not aligned on how to approach certain things. I don't need a snide remark after every interaction. I'm sure you are not always telling me the full story. I KNOW that spoon always in the sink with peanut butter on it is yours.

Maybe I should have let it go when I found out you didn't do your chores like you promised. Maybe you should have remembered before you left to go out with your friends.

But I said the wrong thing at the wrong time – and we drifted a little farther apart.

What I've learned about raising three teenagers is there are seasons, just like anything else.

There are periods when I see that someday we will be the best of friends and times when you won't let me anywhere near your world.

There are moments filled with so much love and laughter I know I'll remember them for the rest of my days, and sometimes the words we say to each other bring me to my knees.

There are days we get along so well and I believe I'm getting this parenting thing right, and nights I can feel your wrath from three rooms away.

And here's the thing, dear teenager, I'll probably keep saying the wrong thing.

Because you are changing every day.

Sometimes you are so grown up it takes my breath away, and sometimes you show just how much you still need to learn. There are times you leave our house so confident I think you are about to fly the nest that very day, and nights I sit in your bed while you shed some tears. There are mornings

I think you will take on the world, and evenings I worry about how you will get through the next day.

Sometimes it feels like I'm parenting a different kid, and what worked yesterday doesn't apply today.

So I'll keep stepping into it with you. I'll keep parenting and guiding, and yes, probably saying the wrong thing sometimes, I'll probably say the wrong thing lots of times.

Because even though you change personalities throughout the day, my job is always the same – and despite the words we sometimes use and the mistakes we make and the periods of silence – I'll love you through them all.

But even when I'm saying the wrong thing, at least we're still talking.

And as long as we're doing that, I know we'll be okay on the other side.

31. On the Cusp of Turning Teen

Sometimes she takes my breath away, this beautiful daughter of mine. She has one foot in her childhood, the other poised to jump and fly into this world.

While the past 12 years went by in a flash, she's filled my memories with so much joy and expanded my heart more than I ever knew possible.

She has burst through my front door a million times, shouting "Mommy!" at the top of her lungs and searching for a hug after a long day at school. She's crept into my bed before dawn for snuggles and stolen my heels to prance around her bedroom more times than I can count. She's entertained us with her unique dance moves and taught us that compassion, when least deserved, can change hearts and minds.

And although I've enjoyed nearly every second, it's all gone by so fast – and it seems like I'm losing my grasp.

Because for my sweet daughter and I, we are now standing on the cusp of turning teen.

I can't lie. I've seen the subtle shift occurring. She grabs my hand less and spends time with her friends more. Her bedroom door shuts the moment she walks through it, and grunts and exasperated sighs come frequently at my requests to clean her room or walk the dog or finish her math homework. She can no longer steal my shoes as her feet are now bigger than mine and rolls her eyes when I try to dance with her in the kitchen – although, with enough prodding and the right music, she'll still join me.

But it's not all bad, as we approach 13.

My daughter is kind and gentle when she babysits our neighbors' children, kissing boo-boos like an expert and chasing barefoot toddlers across the lawn, and I see the mother she may be one day.

She works hard in school and sports and friendships, and I recognize her unlimited potential. She uses her Starbucks gift cards to buy me a latte and will help to fix my hair, and I see our future filled with shopping trips and catch-up conversations in coffee houses.

And I'm taken aback when I see her passion for solving the injustices in this world and her desire to help others and her admonishment for the plastic straws I use to drink my iced tea because don't I remember watching that documentary about the sea turtles? And I know she will change this world for the better.

Sometimes I don't recognize this woman-child standing before me at almost 13, with gangly arms and perfectly styled hair and legs that go down to there. Sometimes I only see a chubby baby swaddled in a pink blanket, a 3-year-old in pigtails with a feathered boa wrapped around her neck carrying her lovey everywhere she goes, an eight-year-old in overalls saving spiders from their demise, a young girl emerging into a woman right before my eyes.

It is a confusing time for both of us.

She is both a hurricane and the calm in our house, simultaneously wreaking joy and havoc wherever she goes. She is moody in one moment and the voice of reason the next. She craves some independence and control, yet still needs my attention and touch. She sheds tears, so many tears, in frustration and anger and contempt and sadness. And in the darkest moments, she lashes out at me – her safe haven – for all that's wrong in her world.

When I feel like my heart will break from the thought of what never will be again, I hear her belly laugh echoing through the halls, and I look deep into the same gray-blue eyes I stared at for hours on end in a small, stark hospital room nearly thirteen years ago.

In that moment, when I didn't think it was possible, when I'm stunned at how this is the same creature who once slept cradled in my arms, my heart inflates back up as I look at my daughter standing before me.

Because she's on the cusp of turning teen.

And I can't wait to see what comes next.

32. REMEMBER THIS FEELING

D ear daughter:
    Remember this feeling.

Remember this time when you were part of something special.

Remember when others cheered you on for doing your best despite that they desperately wanted what you had.

Remember who carried you when you fell short, when you struggled, when you felt like you disappointed others.

This is what life is supposed to look like – supporting one another, holding each other up, screaming the loudest for someone else's success. Even when you weren't successful. Especially when you weren't as successful.

Remember that success is not a limited commodity. There is enough room at the top for all of us in our own unique ways.

Remember that someone else's journey can look different than your own, and that's not an affront to you.

Remember that you can set the tone for how others see victory, and you can set the tone for how others see defeat.

Always use competition to be your best self instead of how you judge yourself against others.

Always be gracious when you lose, but be even more gracious when you win.

Always know that you can't control what others do, but you can always control how you react to it.

And remember, dear daughter, that sometimes the fastest way to the top is by reaching back for the hand of the person behind you and pulling them up, too

Remember this time.

This is how life should look. You can make it happen.

33. STAY IN YOUR LANE

Dear daughters:
   Keep looking straight ahead. Stay in your lane.

I know it's tempting to look right at the girl who may have fancier clothes, or look left at the kid who got a better grade, but keep looking ahead.

Keep your eye on YOUR prize.

Try not to compare yourself to others. You didn't start in the same place. You probably won't end in the same spot, either.

Comparison is not a measurement that is ever accurate. It never tells the truth. It is a thief – of joy, of satisfaction, of peace.

You're going to feel envy sometimes. It's only natural. You'll feel it when you see that photo on Instagram or hear of that accomplishment someone else received.

But don't let it define who you are. Don't let it stop you from celebrating someone else's success. Don't let it hold you back from chasing your dreams.

Social media is like throwing gas on a comparison flame. It exponentially increases the information about people that we're exposed to and will force you to assess against a situation where you don't have context.

Don't let someone else's highlight reel tell you who you are.

Keep your eyes straight ahead, dear daughters. Keep working on your best self. Keep doing what you love, even if you're still learning, even if you're not the best, especially when you're not the best.

Focus on relationships that nourish you. Seek out people who encourage you. Find groups that share your deepest beliefs.

And remember, a stable sense of self comes from thinking about who you are absent any feedback. That means no amount of likes or grade or achievement defines how you think about what type of person you are.

Keep your eyes straight ahead, and be grateful for what you have. I know it's hard.

But the path to happiness and joy and peace will never be on someone else's road.

You have to learn to get there yourself.

34. You Have to Show Up for Your Friends

Dear Daughters:

Make sure you show up for your friends. It's more important than you think.

Show up for the important things, like milestone birthdays and weddings and baby showers.

And show up when they need you, but don't want to ask, like during a tough break up or when they suddenly lose their job or their parent dies.

Make sure you return the call when their voice cracks in the voicemail because they are exhausted from staying up with a newborn three nights in a row. Make sure to send a text letting them know you are thinking about them when their kid goes into surgery or is waiting for a college decision. Make sure you ask about their ailing mom and their struggling marriage and their dreams that always seem just beyond their reach.

When you're married with kids, show up to that girls' weekend even though the logistics seem impossible. Make that extra two-hour drive to stop in and see a friend. Drop off that book you think she'll like or share that meme you think she'll love.

Dear daughters, the most important thing you will do in this life is showing up for the ones you love. Trust me on this.

When you were younger, you asked, "Why do I have to brush all my teeth when no one sees the ones in the back?"

I answered, "You don't have to brush all your teeth. Just the ones you want to keep."

Friendship is the same way. If you only work on the people right in front of you, the rest of your relationships will decay.

So you need to show up.

Because one day, life will happen. You may find out that your child has a debilitating illness or your partner has an affair. You could be in a horrible accident or face a devastating health diagnosis. You may have to relocate your family to a faraway place or decide what to do with an ailing parent.

You might sink into the darkness of depression and anxiety. You might lose yourself in the depths of motherhood. You might face unfathomable grief or distress or despair the likes you've never experienced.

And just when you think you have nowhere to turn, a hand reaches towards you and pulls you out. They reach and pull you out because they showed up – as you always have for them.

You have to brush all your teeth, dear daughters. Trust me on this.

Show up for your friends. Make sure they know you care. Be the friend you want in return every chance you get.

Because life is about showing up for the ones you care about, and everything else can wait.

35. I Was Once the Mom to Little Girls

Once was the mom to little girls who I dressed in cute matching outfits with sweet bows tied firmly in their hair. My house was filled with high-pitched squeals and dress-up clothes and pink and purple everything.

I once was the mom who prayed to make it through to 7:30 p.m. each night and that they might sleep until 7 a.m. the next day, although they always seemed to wake before my alarm. I cried because I was so exhausted. I cried because of frustration. I cried because they brought me so much joy.

I once was the mom who let her tiny daughters prance around in her stilettos for their living room fashion shows and wear tutus at soccer practice and only have one treat a day. I read thousands of bedtime books and let them watch too much TV and yelled too often.

I once was the mom who had little hands attached everywhere, pulling my hair, grasping my hand, and tugging at my heart every single moment. There never seemed enough of me to go around, there never seemed enough time, there never seemed enough sleep.

And just when I thought I couldn't get through one more day, things got a little easier. Then a little harder. Again and again.

They became more independent. They became more opinionated. They became more empathetic and emotional and passionate and fun. I cried because I was exhausted with worry. I cried because I was frustrated by their behavior. I cried because they brought me so much joy.

Until one day, I opened my eyes to mother for another day, and two 18-year-olds stared back at me.

I am no longer the mom of little girls who need me to tie their shoes and brush their long hair and feed them snacks throughout the day.

They are making their own choices, carving out their paths, planning out their dreams. My house is quiet most of the time while they spend their time away from me more. My days are filled with waiting for them to need me and doing what I can to help in the background. I wonder what it will be like when they aren't here next year.

I still worry. I still have hopes and dreams for them. I still cry out of exhaustion and frustration and pride.

But I was once the mother of little girls who grew up right before my eyes. And I was lucky enough to watch it happen, to feel the hurt and the joy and the tired, to love them with all my heart.

I once was the mother of little girls.

What an amazing gift they gave to me.

36. PEACHES

One of the hardest lessons to teach my girls is that no matter what you do, no matter how hard you try to do what's right, no matter your intent, sometimes people just don't like you.

As my mom told me, you can be the ripest, juiciest peach in the box, but sometimes people just don't like peaches.

And I've lived by that motto for most of my adult life. I try to remember that what other people think of me isn't any of my business. I know that I can only control my own thoughts and responses and determine my own worth. I try to lead with compassion at every single juncture.

One day, my daughter came home and said that a girl had walked past her in gym class and bluntly said in front of everyone, "I don't know what it is, but I just don't like you."

I laughed out loud when she relayed the story because it sounded absurd. "Well, at least you know where you stand," I said.

But while it is hard to know that someone doesn't like you, it's even worse when they go out of their way to disparage and discredit and tear you down in front of others. As someone who puts herself out there on the Internet, I know this all too well.

And I wish I had handled that moment with my daughter differently.

Because I forgot what that felt like.

I forgot the pain associated with the exclusion and talking behind the back and judgment.

I forgot what it felt like to lose control of a situation, to let someone else tell your story, to define who you are to others.

I forgot the humiliation and anxiety, and sadness that comes along with it all.

If I could go back and talk to my daughter on that day, I would tell her that it's okay when people don't like you, but it doesn't mean that it doesn't hurt.

I would tell her to remember that feeling she had, and try hard never to make another person feel that way.

I would tell her that the only way to combat the negative someone is putting out into the world about you is to focus on the goodness you know is inside of you and to keep putting that goodness out into the world every chance you get.

I would encourage her to be compassionate to the person causing her pain, even when it took every ounce of her strength.

And I would remind her that even when it feels like the whole world is pushing her down, she is so loved. Because there are so many reminders of our faults and insecurities in this world, so we all need to be reminded of the love as well. A lot.

The world is a harsh place, and we often don't know where we truly stand with one another. In fact, we usually do not stand on equal footing at all.

All we can do is try to put out our best, give some grace, and try to be better tomorrow – especially when we feel the worst.

Be kind whenever you can, friends. Especially when you feel hurt. The person on the other end may need it more than you know.

And love hard.

37. This is 15

This is 15.

15 is early mornings at school and late-night studying.

15 is sleeping any chance she gets and waking up at the last possible second.

15 is eye rolls at jokes she used to find funny and exasperated sighs every time I say no.

15 is starting to understand what's going on in the world today, and thinking of ways to solve it. 15 also likes to binge-watch Outer Banks for nine hours straight.

15 is all legs, messy buns, and big sweatshirts. 15 can also look like a full-fledged woman when she wants, which is both terrifying and beautiful.

15 thinks she knows everything. 15 also asks where to place the stamp on an envelope and how to spell Wednesday.

15 will watch all the best 80s movies with you and then ask questions about your youth. You will

feel closer than ever and that you're doing something right. The next morning she will tell you that you don't understand her life and act like she wants nothing to do with you.

15 will remember every song lyric and TikTok dance but will always forget to pick up her room or put the cup in the dishwasher. You will remember that you also did that at 15, although it doesn't make it any less annoying.

15 makes you apologize to your own mom for when you were 15.

15 no longer finds boys icky and may even have a boyfriend who she wants to spend all her time with. 15 causes you to have an ongoing eye twitch.

15 knows how to hit you where it hurts and strikes in the jugular. 15 is also learning how to apologize and mean it.

15 has one foot in her childhood and the other poised to fly.

15 gives you such a sense of pride that you feel your heart will burst. When 15 hurts, you've never known pain quite like it.

15 will cry in your arms. 15 will push you away. 15 can make you cry.

When 15 wants to spend time with you, you don't care what she wants to do. You'll take her presence any chance you can get.

15 is a firecracker constantly on the verge of an explosion. You never know if it will be a beautiful glow of light or noise so loud it will shake you to your core.

15 needs her mom more than ever. 15 will never admit she needs her mom.

15 can cook a full meal, do the laundry, and is learning how to drive (which seems impossible since she was just in her Barbie jeep yesterday). 15 will have accidents doing all those things. 15 looks responsible but still has a lot to learn.

15 is planning for the future. 15 is also nervous and stressed and anxious about it.

It's hard to be 15. It's also pretty awesome to be 15.

15 is a walking contradiction.

As I look at my 15, I remember a squishy baby who always wanted to eat, kept me up late at night, and constantly made a mess. Everything and nothing has changed during those 15 years.

15 is a challenge, a struggle, a fight.

15 is glorious. And I wouldn't change a thing.

15 makes me sad about what is gone and excited for what comes next.

I couldn't love 15 more.

38. A MOTHER NEVER HAS ENOUGH TIME

She slept right next to my bed every night for months, just close enough so I could reach out and touch her tiny body wrapped snuggly in blankets from her grandmothers. I could have moved her into her own room earlier, but she was my last baby, and I knew enough to appreciate the little coos she made in her sleep and relish the warmth of her body nestled against mine.

A mother can never have enough time.

She spent her infant and toddler years attached to me either in a baby carrier or on my hip or in a stroller. Her twin sisters, only 16 months older, didn't quite understand that she was breakable, so it was easier to keep her on me than risk anything happening to her, so her title of mama's girl was quickly cemented. Because watching three babies was daunting for even the most skilled grandmother, she came with me wherever I went – on short trips to the grocery store and longer ones for weddings and funerals. She lights the room up wherever she goes and is still a fun companion.

A mother can never have enough time.

Through the years I've watched her heart grow as fast as her long, lean body. Her first instinct is always compassion, whether it's on the field, in the classroom, or at home. I see how she carries the weight of the world on her slight shoulders, but I also see how her bravery grows in lockstep with her years. I have no doubt she will change the world.

A mother can never have enough time.

And last night I said goodnight to a child, my baby, and woke up to a smiling 17-year-old. She towers over me and her feet are too big for my shoes, and although I feel like I did not waste one minute with her, although I feel like I did all the things and was at all the places, it still isn't enough.

A mother can never have enough time.

Now, as I watch the young girl sitting at my kitchen counter eating a birthday eclair and laughing at her dad's jokes, I can also see the young woman she is becoming. And I know the time we spend together under one roof is heading to a close. She has big hopes and big dreams, and she is so ready to go after them.

I find myself praying I get to see the rest of her story unfold. I hope she has beautiful experiences completing her education and finds lifelong friends. I wish for her to find a partner to share her life with who is caring and loving. I want to see her have children of her own.

It doesn't matter if you only know you are pregnant for a moment or if you live until you are one hundred. It doesn't matter if you stayed at home with your kids every second of every day or only saw them for a few hours because of work. It doesn't matter if you adopted them in their teens or used fertility drugs or if it was a planned or unplanned pregnancy.

It doesn't matter if your heart is grateful for every moment of messy parenting or if you get frustrated with the chaos. It doesn't matter if your baby has babies of their own or if you're holding your newborn in your arms just after you delivered her.

When you see how swiftly time moves, when you feel the shift in your relationship, when you know that a part of your life, that part of your identity, is changing and coming to an end, it is gut-wrenchingly beautiful.

And although I know we have so much of her story left to write together, it is bittersweet knowing we also can't go back to where we were.

A mother can never have enough time.

39. THIS IS WHAT LOVE LOOKS LIKE

To my three daughters, don't be fooled by what the world says is love.

Don't let the world or social media or a magazine cover tell you what love looks like.

Don't fall into the trap that love is measured in the size of a ring or how much you spend on a vacation or the type of car someone owns.

Don't get caught up with someone who only talks about your looks or your weight or your clothes.

Don't get sucked into professions on social media or late-night whispers or apologies after a fight.

Don't fall for a person whose words and actions don't align.

Watch how a potential partner treats their parents, waiters, or delivery person. Observe if they lose their temper over little things. Listen to how they speak when someone makes a mistake.

Remember how they talk about others when they aren't in the room – because you won't always be in the room.

Grandiose gestures are great. Flowers on special occasions are sweet. Compliments can make you feel warm and fuzzy inside.

Temporarily.

But this, dear daughters. This is what love looks like.

Love is getting up an hour early to shovel snow off the driveway so your kids can get to school.

Love is getting the brakes checked on the car before a big road trip or teaching your teen how to change a tire or iron dresses before a big event.

Love is offering the delivery man a bottle of water on a hot day and helping a neighbor move a couch and rescuing a baby bird from a basement well.

Love is doing the dishes most nights to show that housework doesn't fall on only one person's shoulders in a relationship.

Love is admitting you are wrong – and owning your mistakes.

Oftentimes, we mistake the words we want to hear for love, and that can be a grave mistake.

We see what we want to see, make excuses for what makes us uncomfortable.

But this, my dear daughters, is what love looks like.

Don't forget it.

40. You Don't Have to Have It All Figured Out

D ear Senior:
    I don't care what the world says, you don't *have* to have it all figured out in your last year of high school.

You don't have to know the plan for the rest of your life.

You don't have to feel pushed in a certain direction.

You don't have to give up being a kid, being silly, being young.

You don't have to become an adult just yet solely because of a number you turned on the calendar.

The world may be telling you that you need to know who you want to be when you grow up, but the truth is, many of us adults are still trying to figure that out.

You aren't being left behind. There are no benchmarks for where you should be at this point, no social milestones you need to meet just because your peers are doing them.

Fight against the urge to conform and make choices based on your values and what you deem important. Decisions about sex and drugs and alcohol should be made because you feel ready, not because you've hit a certain age.

You don't have to take on a lot of responsibilities just yet, but you have to be responsible for yourself. You need to own your decisions, your actions, and your mistakes. You need to try and learn from them, but they don't have to define you for the rest of your life.

You're in the last stage of adolescence, but it's okay to know that you have so much left to learn. Don't feel embarrassed to reach out for help, don't feel like you need to know it all, and never think that you are alone in this world.

You can change your mind about all the things. You can explore different careers and interests and friends. There is no one path for everyone.

As you figure out who you want to be in this world, strive for connection – to people, to passions, to art, to anything that brings you peace and contentment. Work hard at creating deeper relationships with friends and family and finding gratitude for the little things.

But please don't try to fill a happiness void in your life with another tangible such as food, alcohol, drugs, shopping, etc. These are short-term fixes and will never solve your problems.

You don't have to make decisions to fit in a certain box. Fight off feelings of guilt and inadequacy and the desire to please.

You have to let go of the idea of perfection and see the beauty in the chaos of your life because you can't try to control everything either (trust me on this one), which only leads to disappointment.

You don't need to have everything planned out just because you're a senior. Just because one thing is coming to a close doesn't mean your plan has to be perfect for this next phase.

You don't need to know what the rest of your life will look like. Oftentimes the greatest joys come from the unknown, the surprises, the things you didn't even know you wanted.

Just keep working on finding out who you are, and more importantly, who you want to be. Learn how to love yourself, and you'll learn to love your life no matter what that looks like.

And I'll be there with you every step of the way.

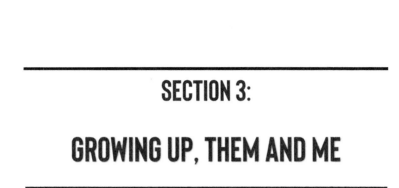

SECTION 3:

GROWING UP, THEM AND ME

INTRODUCTION

With three kids only sixteen months apart, I ran a tight ship in my house in the early years.

My husband traveled quite a bit, so the only way I survived was to stick to a serious schedule. I was relentless at keeping to a naptime and mealtime and bedtime routine because feeling in control was the way I could manage the chaos.

And we survived, and even thrived.

I was proud of how I could manage our family. Maybe even a little smug.

Then, out of nowhere, the pre-teen years hit, and they hit *hard*.

I truly struggled. Between my daughters' newfound attitudes and opinions on everything and quest for independence, I did not handle it well.

I became short-tempered. I was constantly anxious. I started only seeing the bad behavior in my kids instead of their so many beautiful qualities.

I was frustrated and nitpicking and probably a teensy-weensy bit sensitive.

Okay, I was completely overly sensitive about everything.

My tweens were bringing out the worst in me, and I was bringing out the worst in them.

Something needed to change.

Trying to alter my daughters' behaviors, moods and attitudes was not working, so one day in the middle of another yelling match, it finally dawned on me.

How could my daughters grow up knowing what healthy behavior looked like if I wasn't willing to act like a grown-up?

At that moment, I realized that I shouldn't try to change them, but what I could work on, what I could control, what I could improve, was *me*.

It sounds simple when I write it down on paper, but it's taken years of soul-searching for me to find some peace in parenting. I needed to let go of things outside of my control, understand that the teen years are about learning experiences, and have a relentless belief in the goodness of my three beautiful, amazing daughters.

And gratitude. Loads and loads of gratitude for it all.

And when I focused on all that good, I started to see it again in my kids at every juncture, the good, the bad and the typical teenage angst.

What follows on the next few pages are the lessons I've learned while growing up with my three teens. I may have given them life, but they certainly taught me how to live it well.

41. You Can't Uncrack an Egg

My hands wrap tighter around the steering wheel of my silver minivan, and I feel my body turn to steel-like armor, attempting to protect itself from the barbs coming from the back seat.

I remind myself not to engage. She's tired, you're tired. Hormones, definitely for her, possibly for me, are invading this conversation that is starting to take a nosedive.

The familiar feeling of frustration spreads throughout my body as I listen to my daughter complain. I try to control my temper as she tells me she forgot something at school again. She snaps nastily when I ask if she finished something at home, admonishing me for not trusting her.

I don't like the words I am hearing, nor the attitude that drips into every conversation, no matter how innocuous the subject matter is. I worry about the person she is becoming, wonder where I went wrong.

"Don't respond," I chant to myself. "Be the adult."

Her tone is laden with disdain, my nerves fray. I tell myself that this is a phase, remind myself of her positive attributes, which are many.

I attempt to change the conversation, trying to avoid the minefield topics that always result in a lecture from me and eyeball rolls from her. I struggle with steering her away from the negativity. I ask questions, she coldly remarks, I accuse, she defends. The game is the same and endless each time.

I finally crack, like the first hit of an egg. Anger oozes slowly out at first, then dumps out of me with no end in sight.

I have an out-of-body experience. I hear the words coming out of my mouth but they don't sound like mine. They are loud and accusatory. Mean-spirited and judgmental. Not appropriate for a conversation with a young girl.

Yet they pour out of me fast and furious for several minutes. She sits in the back seat, looking out the window, her jaw set. I can almost feel the hard clench of her teeth.

The last traffic signal before our house turns a dull yellow and I slam on my brakes to slow down. My words and vehicle freeze simultaneously as the light turns red.

Stop.

We're both silent as I drive the last half of a mile home and pull into our dimly lit garage. She gets out first, and I watch her tiny frame walk quickly into the house.

I sit by myself, hands still gripping the steering wheel tightly, and wonder: "How did I get here?"

I replay the scene in my mind from beginning to end. It is not pretty. I am not proud.

I want to take the words back, but you can't *uncrack* an egg.

I inhale deeply, trying to quash the tears that brim my heavy eyes. I feel defeated. I feel ashamed.

How can something I love the most in this world bring out the worst in me? How do I bring out the worst in her?

I slowly get out of the car and enter the door of our home, the safe haven for my family.

I putter around, keeping my eyes cast downward. Five people are in the kitchen, all stealing glances at each other to see who is brave enough to slice the cord of tension in the room first. There is no banter or giggles.

It is not an uncommon occurrence lately for the air to be heavy when my daughter and I walk into a room. It is not a secret that our relationship is strained, and it is a weight each person in our household must bear.

I put plates in the dishwasher and wipe crumbs off the counter, my mind occupied with the events that transpired moments before. My husband catches my eyes and lifts his eyebrows. He is painfully aware of how fast my daughter and I can go off the rails, bearing witness to the event on more than one occasion.

I nod my head up and down with pursed lips, signaling to him that yes, it happened again. I mouth the word 'later', hoping he understands I can't go there just yet.

I head to the couch, and flop down, hoping the brown leather will swallow me whole, taking away the person that lost it on the little girl in the car.

I flip on the television and toss the remote to the side. First one member, then another, and another joins me in the family room as we zone out for a few minutes before bedtime, sitting together, yet alone.

I hear my daughter behind me, shuffling papers and packing her bag for school the next day.

I close my eyes, willing my body to go back in time.

I startle when I feel the warmth of a person sitting suddenly beside me. Without turning my head, I look at the sock-clad feet of my daughter and marvel that we nearly wear the same size. I take a deep breath and inhale her familiar smell of sweat and outside. I slowly move my arm up and around to the back of the sofa, like a young boy trying to make a move on his date.

I exhale when surprisingly she leans into the crook of my body, leaning her head into my chest. I wrap my arm around her shoulder, cautiously bringing her closer to me.

We sit as one, connected, for a few beautiful moments. Our breaths are synchronized, our souls aligned. We are better without words, our relationship stronger minus conversation. At least for now.

When the show is over, she slowly stands up, turns to face me, and says, "I'm going to get ready for bed. And I'll go put my laundry away."

I look deep into her eyes and see a reflection of my own. I recognize she is waving a metaphorical white flag, so I smile and simply say, "Thanks."

There will be no resolution tonight, no comfortable denouement to this chapter.

But I comfort myself knowing that neither of us is giving up, and my heart tells me we will somehow come out on the other side of this storm.

I drag my weary body off the couch and notice my daughter's library book sitting on the counter.

I decide not to make her come downstairs to put it away tonight. I decide not to remind her she needs to be more responsible for her things or more organized.

Instead, I decide to give grace to my daughter, instead of a lecture, encouragement instead of complaints. It is the best that I can do this night.

I grab a pink Post-it note out of a drawer and write, "I am proud to be your mother. Love, Mom," and stick it hastily on the front cover of the young adult novel.

I shove the book in her overcrowded backpack, and leave my hand on it for a moment, sighing with relief that I'm ending the night with her better than the last.

I can't *uncrack* an egg. But I can try to treat the next one with care.

42. BLUE HAIR AND PICKING BATTLES

I let my 12-year-old daughter get blue hair today. More of a turquoise, really.

And my 13-year-old went with purple.

When they first brought up the notion of coloring their hair several months ago, I tabled the idea with a, "We'll see."

They were both pleasantly surprised that I didn't immediately say 'no way', so they kept casually bringing it up here and there.

I tried to think of a good reason not to do it.

There are no school rules against it. It doesn't require any additional maintenance. They were supplementing the cost of it out of their birthday/Christmas money.

Yet, I was having a hard time wrapping my head around it, mainly because there was no way my parents would have allowed it. My conservative father blew his gasket when I double-pierced my ear in 11th grade, so blue hair would never be an option.

I also loved their hair the way it was. It was long and healthy and beautiful.

Sometimes we really have to ask ourselves why we are saying no to a request from our kids.

When I thought about it, there were only two reasons not to do it. It meant I relinquished control over their appearance, and it is something I would never have done at their age.

Both seemed like pretty selfish and silly reasons.

So, I finally made the appointment, and we told our hip colorist that we wanted the tips done, and my daughters walked out with a lot of blue and purple hair.

Whoops.

But they couldn't be happier.

But even more interesting was every woman in the place stopped to tell me that I was a good mom for letting them do this.

It seemed odd to me, until one older mom remarked, "Young people have so little say over their lives, and when we give them a bit, we lend some balance to the relationship. Trust me, you are smart to let them do this."

That stopped me in my tracks.

So on the drive home, when the girls were profusely thanking me, I told them this: "Remember that you thought I was going to say no, we discussed it, and then we came to a solution together. Before you ever go off and do something stupid, remember we can always talk about it first – even if you think I'll say no. Give me the same chance I gave you."

They nodded their heads and flipped their hair, and it warmed my heart to see them so happy because of such a small thing, knowing that we will probably have to tackle something bigger tomorrow.

Learning how to pick and choose our battles in the tween years can set us up for more peaceful teen years.

Everyone who has raised a teenager talks about learning how to pick and choose their battles, but I've always struggled with figuring out which ones to pick. What seems important today can seem silly tomorrow when something bigger comes along.

There is a constant tug-of-war between parents who want to keep their babies safe and teenagers who are desperate to fly free.

What I'm learning is any time that I'm just trying to prove to my teens who is in charge, we end up in the weeds. To raise a productive, respectful adult, you have to treat your big kid respectfully.

That means being flexible to understand their different perspective – no matter how ridiculous it sounds to you.

Don't get me wrong, I still have rules and boundaries and guidelines that are non-negotiable. I still give consequences when they do something wrong. And I still sometimes lose my mind when I see my daughter's disaster of a room, even though I keep telling myself that it's not a battle worth fighting right now.

But it also means that we have to let our kids grow up a little and start making decisions for themselves, with some guidance of course. That means instead of constantly saying, "I know what's best for you," instead we have to start asking our kids, "What do you think is best for you?"

That is HARD.

Sometimes the growing-up phase from childhood to teen happens fast, and you can feel like you have whiplash. It's tempting to want to throw on the emergency brake just to catch your breath.

But as long as your child is making sound, thoughtful decisions and not engaging in risk-taking behavior, sometimes you have to start following their lead.

Did I mention that this is hard?

I always have to ask myself: "What kind of relationship do I want with my teen, and will this battle get me there?"

I'm finding that when I am open and honest with my young teens about my concerns about something and don't let my fear get the best of me, we have some of our most productive discussions. Teens appreciate when you are forthright and tell the truth, and sometimes, if you are lucky, they return the favor by being honest with you.

I don't think I'm a good mom because I let my girls turn their hair a different color – but I do think I got parenting right today by listening to my kids and giving them some consideration on something that was important to them.

Today I said yes because I feel certain there will be a lot of 'no's' in the future.

And as the saying goes, hair today, gone tomorrow.

43. Children Are Meant to Be Unfinished

"And don't forget you didn't finish the laundry," I yell defiantly.

I watch the slim profile of my daughter stomp up the stairs, her dark ponytail swinging side to side. I can hear her breathing through her nose, in and out, in and out, like a bull about to charge. I watch as she turns the corner, out of my view. I brace myself, waiting for the door to slam, yet thankfully I hear a quiet click of metal on the wooden frame.

I stand still, one hand clutching the railing, the other clenched so tightly I can feel my unshaped nails indenting my palm. I can feel the tension in my right shoulder blade. I slowly release the bite I have on my lower lip, my weak attempt at trying to keep my rage locked up inside.

Today's argument with my young teen daughter is no different from the ones we have almost daily lately. It could be about finishing her homework or putting her dishes away or completing her chores. Sometimes it's about her attitude with her sisters or her tone with me or her inability to finish anything she starts. My lectures seem to be on a continuous loop with no end in sight.

Each morning I wake with a new resolve to be a better mother, one who does not nag so much or finds innovative ways to motivate her kids.

But somewhere during the day, I watch as my daughter refuses to follow our house rules, chooses to ignore what needs to be done.

Sometimes we let her fail and succumb to the consequences of her forgetfulness. Sometimes we help her organize her day. Sometimes I remember that everyone needs a little help now and again.

And sometimes we seem to make progress, only to go two steps back the next day.

"Be more laid back," I tell myself. "Not everything is a big deal or a teachable moment. Pick your battles."

But as she gets closer to adulthood each and every day, I worry. Will she learn the skills she needs to succeed? Will she live a life to her potential or will she merely get through a day?

I am startled as I see her small body appear on the stairs again, stomping down step by step, avoiding my eyes. She holds a white laundry basket in her hand, and I bite my tongue as I watch it bump into the spindles on my staircase.

Her shoulder bumps into mine as she struggles to turn the corner, and the metaphor is not lost on me.

My relationship with my daughter is like an unfinished chore.

Something you don't want to deal with, but you know needs attention. I want her to be finished now, so the petty arguments and fights can be done, and we can move on to the good stuff.

But what I often forget is children are meant to be unfinished. Children are meant to continue improving and learning and finding their way.

What sometimes feels like a chore instead should be approached like sculpting a masterpiece, letting the clay form where it is supposed to under my hands. I will try to slow down the process however, knowing this beautiful piece of art doesn't need to be finished just yet.

I have to fight the urge to 'fix' my daughter, fight the desire to change who she is. I have to fight the pressure to teach her everything I want her to know before she leaps into the world on her own.

Because children are meant to be unfinished.

But her laundry, well, that still needs to get done.

44. Don't Let Them Change You

My daughter laughed as she said it, but I could see the hurt in her eyes.

"She just walked right past me, pointed her finger, and said, 'I don't like you, not at all.' And then she kept right on going."

"What did you say?" I asked. "Did you do anything?"

"Nope," she replied. "I'm just going to avoid her."

The people-pleaser in me thought that was a wise decision. I mean, being a teen is hard enough – who wants to engage in more drama?

A few weeks later, my other daughter and I sat in line, waiting to go into a school program. Another mom and daughter we know from school sidled up behind us.

The mom and I chatted, but my normally talkative daughter stayed mute. In fact, the two girls smiled and looked pleasant, but barely looked at each other. It was borderline rude.

When I asked her about it later, she shared that the other young girl didn't like her. "Why would you say that? I mean, don't you guys have a lot of the same friends?"

"Trust me, Mom, I KNOW she doesn't like me. She's told a bunch of people, so I just don't know how to act around her."

That's when it hit me. My kids are great about being kind to others, but they become shrinking violets when another person doesn't like them. They become unrecognizable.

And that's not okay.

I need to get my girls comfortable with the fact that they will not be liked by everyone – but more importantly, that it shouldn't change who they are as a person and how they behave.

I wanted to tell my daughters that these girls must be jealous of them for some reason or insecure with their own lives. I wanted to tell them that girls are just mean or that their opinions don't matter a bit. I wanted to make my kids feel better.

But, at the end of the day, I don't want my daughters to spend any time rationalizing the behavior of anyone else. I want them to feel confident that they are good people who try to do the right thing, and that is enough. Everything else is out of their hands.

The end.

So, I shared this powerful truth with my kids. "Not everyone is going to like you, and that is okay."

But then I added, "But don't you dare let anyone change your behavior because of it. Be confident in who you are."

We discussed the situations where they could have acted a bit differently. We talked about how sometimes the easiest way to ease the tension is by merely saying, "Hello." We discussed how avoiding people is unnecessary if you feel confident that you did nothing wrong. We chatted about different ways to engage in uncomfortable situations, and even what to do if someone comes at them in a vicious way.

A few weeks later, I dropped my daughter off at school to meet some friends. Sitting on the park bench surrounded by a few other middle schoolers was the young girl she couldn't talk to a few weeks back.

I watched as she looked over, gave a beautiful smile, and said, "Hey guys! What's up?" as she walked in through the entrance gate.

The young girl, who didn't speak a word to her previously, held up her hand and gave a smile and a nod.

As I pulled away from the curb, I thought progress may be slow and shallow, but it's progress nonetheless. And this mom will take it.

45. THE LIE THAT BUILT A BRIDGE

My young teenage daughter lied to me the other day. It wasn't a whopper, but it was one in an ongoing saga of untruths we've dealt with over the past few years.

So, instead of punishing her, I took her to Starbucks for a sugar-laden coffee drink.

Let me explain. We've cracked down on every mistruth she's told before. We grounded her and took her phone. We've talked (ad nauseam) about earning trust. We've argued and pleaded. We've had her work toward earning our trust back.

We've done all the things.

Because trusting your teen – especially in this day and age – is important. And if we can't trust her with the little things, how can we trust her with the big things?

How can we put her behind the wheel of a car or believe she'll call us when she's in trouble or tell us if someone is hurting her? How can we send her off to college or on trips without us?

So, the other day, when she got caught, I was exasperated. I was at the end of my rope. I was over it.

When I confided in a friend, she stopped me in my tracks when she quietly said, "Don't you remember how much we lied to our parents growing up?"

"But that was different," I immediately responded.

And she laughed because, of course, I already saw the irony. "Your teen will lie to you," she said. "About something. It's inevitable."

So, we talked about the reasons why I lied to my parents when I was growing up. Of course, it was because I felt like they could not relate to my life. And that I knew they would say no to me. And I was embarrassed to tell them certain things about boys or my friends or where I was going. And that I didn't want them to be disappointed in me.

And my personal favorite, I simply didn't want to receive a lecture (apparently, psychologists call this conflict avoidance).

I was different from my parents, though – except lying between teenagers and their moms and dads has been going on since the dawn of time.

In my mind, I created a personal narrative that justified my lying to my parents back in the day way more than my daughter's lying to me now. I said to myself, "I didn't lie about small things," or, "I talked to them about the important stuff," but the truth is, sometimes I lied simply because it was easier.

I was caught in an ongoing circle of Hell with my daughter and the lies. I was looking for them all the time. I constantly asked if she was telling me the truth. I had to stop myself from checking up on her all the time.

This was not the relationship I wanted with one of my kids.

So, when I caught her in the last fib, instead of my normal flipping out or incessant lecture or off-the-cuff punishment, I told her we would talk about it the next day.

After she came home from a long school day, I loaded her up in the car and took her to the closest Starbucks. I let her buy whatever she wanted, and we sat down.

We chatted about her day and the plans for the weekend. She told me she was frustrated with her math teacher, and I talked about a meeting that went wrong.

And then I told her that I used to lie to my parents, too, sometimes. I told her how lying got me in more trouble than it was worth, how it hurt my relationship with my parents when I got caught, and now, looking back, how I could have done things differently.

I explained that I wish I had more courage with my dad, and that I believed my mom when she told me I could talk to her, and that she often knew I was lying even when she didn't say anything.

I then talked about the different ways I wanted to trust her moving forward. I wanted to believe that she could be trusted behind the wheel of the car, out on dates, or with her friends, but that trust was a two-way street.

And I told her that no one can ever be trusted if they aren't given opportunities to be trustworthy.

I explained that I wanted to take away some of the reasons she felt the need to lie. I would back off on the barrage of questions and lectures if she promised to be a little more open and honest. I told her that I wanted to be there to teach and guide instead of punish and blame.

There was a halfway point, but we'd both have to stretch ourselves to get there.

She nodded her head and didn't say much, but my heart felt a little lighter. I've found out lately that so much of the suckiness in the teenage years is getting caught in a cycle, doing the same thing over and over again. Take away the friction, and oftentimes you can move on.

There is nothing more difficult in these challenging teenage years than finding the balance of your kid, knowing there will be repercussions for their actions while also keeping an open line of communication.

The end goal is to ensure my daughters always know they can come to me, no matter what. And that we can solve anything over an iced coffee drink.

46. Friction

Last week, I wore my heavy wool socks and my boots to walk the dog on a cold, wet Fall day. In the middle of my two-mile jaunt, I realized my left heel started to hurt. By the time I made it home, I had a blister the size of a quarter on the back of my foot.

A blister happens from friction – constant forceful rubbing.

Last year, my relationship with my young teen daughter was a gigantic blister. We constantly rubbed each other the wrong way.

I was so frustrated with her behavior that I pushed her on everything. Her unkempt room and schoolwork and attitude. Her lack of awareness for others. Her inaction to change.

She started circumventing the truth whenever I confronted her and shutting down. She retreated to her room at every opportunity. She pushed back out of frustration.

Our relationship was a blister, and it was hurting us both.

If you've ever had one, you know your only course of action is to stop doing what caused the blister in the first place. Give the blister some room to heal. Stop the friction from occurring.

I had to wake up every morning and decide if I was going to pressure my daughter that day. Was I going to nag her about her bedroom? Needle her about the chores she didn't do? Take away her phone or ground her for not listening?

Or would my love be more of a soothing balm, healing us both?

I was tired of the constant friction. It was unhealthy for our entire house.

So, I started helping her a bit more. Instead of yelling at her that she forgot to make her lunch – again – I just made it and left it on the counter for her. Instead of engaging when she made a snarky comment, I simply said, "Well, let's just end our conversation on that note," and walked away. Instead of barraging her with questions about school and her friends, I started asking her to hang out with me more for coffee dates or cooking dinner or watching a show.

I didn't let her get away with big things. We have house rules that are non-negotiable. But I made a mental list of what were big things and what were small things, and I realized my list of small stuff was so much longer than I ever thought.

I kept at it for several months. Sometimes I helped her, and sometimes I let her fall. Sometimes I forced a hug so she could physically feel my presence, and sometimes I let her dictate the terms of our relationship. Sometimes I let a terse word or action roll off my back, and sometimes I simply said, "Please leave the room if you are going to behave like this."

And one day, as we hung out baking cookies, I realized my relationship with my daughter didn't hurt anymore. It felt warm and fuzzy, like my favorite pair of wool socks.

We healed the blister by taking away the friction.

Some teens are just harder than others. Some act out because they are frustrated or confused or just so desperate for independence that they only know how to painfully kick you away.

You can fight it with all your might, but know that friction often causes blisters, and some can become pretty bad.

Or you can take the friction away.

I took my dog for a walk yesterday. I wore the same boots, but slipped on a thin pair of socks and wore a few band-aids for good measure.

Oh yeah. My daughter came with me. Just because she wanted to hang out.

47. IT's ALL PERSONAL

Right before I was married, my mom told me that she overheard me speaking to my brother on the phone when he was away at college. I was thirteen and completely full of myself. I went on and on about how my mom embarrassed me, from her clothes to her hair to the type of car we drove. I wanted a 'normal' mom and I wished she would just leave me alone.

I was ready to take on the world, and my parents were just in my way.

I can't recall what spurred that memory for her, but my mother told me she cried for three days after hearing my words. She made a tremendous effort to connect with me and provide the fun teenage years she never had, and even though she knew we were going through typical pains associated with puberty, she didn't know how I truly felt.

As I listened to her words, I felt the heat of shame creep up on my cheeks. Of course, I apologized. I attempted feeble amends for my behavior during those years and claimed that it must have been my hormones.

But even though decades have passed by, and we have an amazing relationship now, I remember feeling that way. I remember feeling embarrassed of my mother and wishing I could be a little 'cooler' than my family could manage.

Luckily, that was a short phase, and it didn't take long for me to realize that I was acting like an idiot, and my mother was a living, breathing saint. God and karma had the last laugh, however, and blessed me with three daughters of my own.

I think about that story a lot when I am in the weeds of parenting three teenage girls, which, to be honest, is every day. I think about how I broke my mother's heart and how she told me she course-corrected a lot based on my attitude toward her.

If I was belligerent, she knew it was often something going on with my friends. She let me get away with a little bit more, then.

If I was exceedingly obedient, she knew I was guilty of something, and she tightened the reigns.

When I lashed out at her, she knew she needed to reel me back in a little tighter.

But to think that I didn't hurt her during these times, to think that she didn't take it personally, well, I could tell by her face that she carries a little bit of that pain with her to this day.

It's this knowledge that frustrates me sometimes when experts say, "Don't take what your teen says or does personally."

I mean, I understand it in theory. They will make bad choices that are not a reflection of your parenting. Sometimes they just want to get a rise out of you. It could just be hormones or 'hanger' or simply them slowly breaking away.

But my relationship with my children is the most personal thing in this world to me, and during this tumultuous time, their words and actions often shatter my heart.

I often tell myself that I'm too emotional, too invested, but I don't know how to parent any other way. I'm not even sure if I would want to.

But instead of telling parents not to take it personally, let's start acknowledging that there are going to be times your teen strikes you where it hurts, perhaps even where you are most vulnerable. Let's start admitting that watching your teen make poor choices is gut-wrenching. Let's start supporting each other through those times when our teens break our hearts.

Because every one of us is going through it, feeling it, trying to figure out what we're doing wrong. And if you're not, consider yourself lucky.

It's all personal.

I'm not glad I hurt my sweet mom, but I'm glad she kept feeling my emotions. I'm glad she didn't respond in kind, and instead parented the kid in front of her at any given moment. I'm glad she called me out when I acted like a brat and lost her temper because I pushed too hard, and coddled me when I needed it most.

She simultaneously felt every emotion as I went through it, and loved me through it all. It was personal to her and part of our story.

I wish the experts would say, "Your teen will break your heart, but I promise you'll survive. In fact, one day, if you're lucky, your relationship will be stronger because you felt it all – the good times and the bad."

Because I'm no expert on raising teens, but that's the one thing I know.

48. SOMETIMES I MISS THE LITTLENESS

When I returned home from walking the dog early this morning, there was no room to put my shoes away in the fancy organizing area I created in my hall closet. The shelves were lined with size 10 cleats and running shoes and 12 pairs of flip-flops.

And for a moment, I went back to when little sandals and Crocs and Velcro sneakers were strewn all over my house.

As I walked into the kitchen, I saw a gigantic mess of plates and pans and cereal bowls in the sink. On the counter was a note from one of my teen daughters saying, "We will clean up when we get home from practice. Promise!"

I was startled when I heard the booming voice of my 14-year-old from upstairs. "Mom, I need more razors. And a bunch of other stuff. Are you going to the store today?"

No one tells you how many toiletries three teen girls go through on a weekly basis – and how expensive it can be. In fact, I feel like all I do is write check after check lately. When someone coined high school as 'the wallet years', they weren't kidding.

Everything in my life with teenagers seems big lately. Big stuff, big messes, big expenses, big problems, big emotions.

And sometimes when I'm in the thick of it, I long for the littleness.

The feel of two small arms around my neck. The excitement of letting them pick out a toy in the Dollar-spot at Target. The little snacks I used to provide every hour. The little feet that used to walk around in my too-big heels.

But then I remember the bigness of my kids has some perks, too.

Like the big responsibilities my girls can now handle, like staying home alone or cleaning up their messes or making their own money.

Or the new relationship I formed with them because they are now big enough to sit in the front seat or watch movies I want to see or buy me a Starbucks with their very own gift card.

Or getting a front-row seat to watch their heart grow bigger every day, with new romances or compassionate gestures or just when they begrudgingly say, "I love you too, Mom" when I drop them off at a practice or friend's house.

Sometimes it's easy to get overwhelmed in a house full of teenagers (or even just one). Everything can just feel so big. Everything can just feel like so much.

And when I long for the little things, the little objects, the little people who have left my home, I just have to remember the big things that are sitting right in front of me.

Because they are pretty great, too.

49. TEENS LIKE TO TRY STUFF ON

My husband bought me a dress for our wedding anniversary, the first time in 25 years that he purchased me a piece of clothing.

I loved the gesture, and I wanted to love the dress, but when I tried it on, I just didn't. It was too tight in all the wrong places, and too loose in others. The length wasn't right.

It just didn't feel like me.

When I modeled it for my husband, of course, he loved it, so for a brief moment, I wanted to love it too to make him happy. But he could see on my face that I felt uncomfortable, and he kindly told me to pick something else out for our upcoming trip.

"Pick something that makes you feel great, and I'll love it," he said.

I enlisted one of my daughters to go with me to pick out a new dress. She loves fashion, so I thought it would be a great way to spend a few hours together.

As we went store to store, I kept recommending clothes for her to try on, and she subtly mumbled that she didn't need a dress like that or that the shorts I recommended wouldn't fit her for some reason.

And I started to get kind of frustrated, but I tried to bite my tongue.

My relationship with my daughter can best be described as rocky. My once easy-going kid has developed an edge that sometimes makes her unrecognizable to me. She is fiercely independent, opinionated, and yes, moody. I always thought she and I had a close bond, but I often feel like her growing up is like constantly ripping off a band-aid.

It often feels like she says no before I even make a suggestion about something. It often feels like she does it for spite. It often feels like my opinion weighs less and less, even when I think she needs it the most.

When we get along, we have so much fun. When we don't, think of two rams butting heads to the death to win back their territory.

Finally in one of the last stores we went into, we found a dress for me that I loved. The fit was perfect, the color was fun, and it made me feel great.

My daughter enthusiastically said, "Mom, that dress is so YOU. I love it."

And that's when it hit me.

It's not that my daughter is rejecting all my suggestions. She's trying stuff on to see what fits.

She's trying on different friendships. She's trying on different hobbies. She's trying on different school subjects and fashion choices and hair. She's trying on different personalities, sometimes multiple ones a day, to see what she likes, to see what makes her comfortable, to find what makes her feel great.

And just like the dress my husband bought me, the one that he thought I would LOVE, what makes my daughter feel great may not be the same as what I would have selected for her.

Of course, deep down, I knew this already. Of course, I knew that she needs to find what makes her feel good, what makes her glow, what makes her love her life.

But watching her face light up when she saw me in the perfect dress reminded me that I always need to light up for what makes her feel good about herself, too.

After we exchanged my dress, I asked her if she would like to go back to any of the stores and try on something she saw that she loved.

Instead, she took me into one that I would probably not have entered on my own. She picked up a pair of jeans and paired it with a shirt that I wouldn't have looked twice at – and of course, she rocked it.

She came out with her head held high and the biggest smile on her face, and another mom came by asking us where we picked out the outfit because she thought her daughter would love it too.

My daughter shyly asked, "Mom, what do you think?"

I replied, "It's perfect. It's so YOU."

50. As Time Goes Through the Hourglass

Recently, I watched from the side as my husband nagged my daughter about putting on more cold-weather gear before soccer practice. She was frustrated because she already planned out what she was going to wear, and he wouldn't stop.

He wasn't wrong. It was cold and wet.

After a few minutes of bickering and near tears, I finally looked at my amazing husband and said, "Stop. She either will bring more clothes, or she'll be cold. She may be miserable, but she's not going to die. We can't go to college with her and remind her to take a coat."

And you may think I'm wise because I'm picking my battles, but to be honest, that's not it.

I only got about an hour that day to spend with her. She left for school early and came home late. I had to run errands and returned home right before she left for practice. When she arrived home, she was so tired that she watched TV with me for 15 minutes, and then she went upstairs to take a shower and go to bed.

I only had 60 minutes total with her yesterday – and I know I didn't give her my full attention that entire time.

I realized that it's not time that's speeding up – it's the amount of time I have with my kids each day that is dwindling.

How do I want to spend that time? Can I pour enough love into her in an hour to get her through the trials of her day?

So, I told my husband to stop needling her about her gear, and when I told him why, he got it too.

I've spent the first 14 years of my daughters' lives teaching them lessons about how to care for themselves. Brush your teeth. Don't forget to floss. Get your homework out of the way so you can relax. Be kind. Pick up after yourself. Help to pick up for others. Here's how to make spaghetti and meatballs.

They already have so many life skills, and now that they are teenagers, it's up to them to choose to use them where I can oversee.

And while I'll keep on teaching them how to survive in this world, set boundaries, and help them to become productive adults, my job now is to encourage them in every way.

I want to use the small amount of time I have each day to make sure my daughters know that they are loved, that I am so proud of them, that they have a safe place to come home to every night.

I want to use my 3600 seconds to help them chase their dreams and talk about their problems and support them when they are stressed.

And I know that we still will have fights about wet towels on the floor and dishes in the sink and why they did not walk the dog, but when I can, I do not want to waste the small amount of time I have with them on these minutiae. I don't want them to tune me out every time I open my mouth. I don't want every conversation to end in tears.

This doesn't mean I let them get away with being slobs or not adhering to their responsibilities

– but the stuff that doesn't matter, the stuff I know they need to figure out on their own? Well, I've covered that.

Our time with our teens is limited, it's moving fast, and it's important. If you have the opportunity to pour some extra love in whatever time you have, do it.

They need it. You need it. And it's really the only thing that matters.

51. I Almost Broke My Daughter's Spirit

There's always one kid who gives you a run for your money, and I almost broke her spirit.

So alike that we butt heads like two rams fighting for the same space.

So different that sometimes we feel like we live on separate planets.

I have a problem with biting my tongue. She likes to have the last word.

Sometimes we both go too far.

And I almost broke her spirit.

It's tough to raise a strong-willed child, especially when you're a strong-willed adult. It's tough to find the line between when to push, when to pull back, and when to let go. It's tough to find the balance of watching her make mistakes while keeping her safe.

Truth be told, I messed up a lot. So did she.

When our relationship was good, it was great. And when we went off the rails, we went a mile off the tracks.

I nitpicked about the small stuff and lost my mind about some of the big things. I needled. I pried. I threatened and yelled.

She dug in sometimes and ignored me on other occasions.

Both of us were wrong, but neither of us was right. But sometimes, I forgot I was the grown-up.

I can't take back some of the words I said to my daughter any more than I can put water back in a hose – but someone once told me that discipline without love equals rebellion, but discipline balanced with grace often grows into respect.

So, I stopped the nitpicking and let her feel like she won sometimes. I gave up control of the things that didn't matter. I gave grace even when it pained me to my core.

I didn't let her walk all over me, but she always knew she was loved.

And sometimes it was so hard.

But when I backed off, I watched her spirit soar in the beautiful ways I knew it could. She became kinder and more considerate and (mostly) easier to get along with. We learned how to enjoy each other and found mutual respect.

Our relationship isn't perfect, but I'm proud of how far we've come.

I almost broke my daughter's spirit, and what a loss to the world that would have been.

52. Walking Towards a Sunrise

I've been walking my young teens to the bus stop. Not all the way, because that would be mortifying for them. I walk them to the end of our block, and they turn right, and I turn left.

Each morning I wake up, make the coffee and putter around the kitchen. The dog wants to go out, but I make him wait a few extra minutes, slowly putting on his harness and leash until my kids are ready to go catch the bus.

And when they are ready to walk out my door into their world, I am ready, too. Because I want that 90 seconds with my kids before they head to school. I *need* it.

I always feel like they are walking away from me lately, headed in a different direction. They spend their days at school and sports practices and friends' houses. And even when they are in my home, under my roof, they still aren't always 'here'. They are on their phones or studying in their rooms or getting ready to leave.

I used to think the pain I felt was natural. Their breaking away from me, the pain of letting go and of what's to come. I know it is what's supposed to happen, but the truth is *I just miss them*.

So, I get to spend a few extra moments with them under the guise of walking my dog. Sometimes our short walk is filled with silence, the crunch of feet on frozen grass the only conversation.

Sometimes it's filled with affirmations and wishing luck on a big test.

And sometimes, when I'm very lucky, it's filled with insight into a life I'm desperate to remain connected to.

This morning, while one of my teen daughters stayed home sick, I started my morning walk with her twin sister. We were only a few steps out of our garage when she grabbed my arm. "Mom, look."

She reached around into her backpack to grab her phone. "Isn't it beautiful? I hate getting up early, but some of the sunrises are awesome."

She snapped some photos and excitedly talked about one day living near a beach and maybe taking a photography class this summer and perhaps she and I could take a trip somewhere so she could practice.

And in a flash, our short walk was done. She gave me a kiss on the cheek and ruffled our dog's head and she was gone with a quick "I love you."

As I watched her narrow frame weighted down with a backpack full of responsibilities walk away from me this morning, it was the first time I felt like she wasn't leaving me, that she wasn't desperate to unhinge herself from my grasp; instead, she was walking towards something beautiful, the sunrise illuminating the next wonderful phase of her life.

And for once, I didn't feel sad letting her go.

I was excited for what is to come for her, eager to see how her life will unfold, even though I know I won't always be a part of it.

I watched her walk off into the morning light, full of brilliant shades of oranges and pinks breaking away from the darkness. I turned left, where the sun hadn't yet touched the evening sky.

The metaphor was not lost on me.

Life is born with a sunrise. I'm grateful I was able to share this one with her.

53. LET THEM EAT CAKE

I spent most of the day yesterday trying to spend some quality time with my three teens. Between cold weather and finals coming up and the stress of college admissions and teenage angst, it's been a lot lately.

And as it happens, I can't help noticing how they morph into their phones a bit more when they are stressed – even worse than just typical 'teenagerdom'.

So, yesterday, we ran some errands and I made them take a walk with me and the dog and we watched a movie and ordered in dinner. We spent an hour at Target looking at hangers and throw pillows. We made hot chocolate at home.

Don't get me wrong. They scrolled in the car or while waiting at the counter.

But mostly, they were present and good-humored about how in-their-face I was for the day.

So, when my youngest decided at 9:30 p.m. she wanted to bake a cake and asked if I wanted to help, my first instinct was to say 'have fun' and head off to bed.

But as I was gathering up my things, my second daughter came downstairs and sat next to me. And then my third.

Before I knew it, there was music playing and laughter and someone made a decision to make green frosting.

In a flash, it was 11:30 p.m., and we were all full of cake.

During those two hours, we talked about some big issues like prejudices and how I was raised in a more socially-conservative household. We talked about little issues, like some divisiveness at school and what teacher they liked the most. We discussed how boxed cakes are awesome and what college is like and hopes and dreams for our futures.

I almost missed it. I almost missed it as I thought we spent the day together and what was there left to say and what left was there to do.

But those activities were all on my terms – and I need to remember that even though the bulk of the day I made my kids trail after me, the parenting gold is when they ask you to do something with them.

That is the sign they're letting you into their world, their comfort zone.

When your teen asks you to do something with them, do it. Don't hesitate.

Listen to the crazy music. Watch the movie they've been dying to see. Learn about the weird technology. Listen to their opinions about issues. Play the video game. Bake the cake – even when it's late.

We all spend a lot of time watching our kids do what they love from the outside, but we still need to work hard to wiggle into the inside.

We make all the rules, so they want to dictate their world a little bit, so when they let you in, don't miss it.

Even if you're a little tired because of it the next day.

54. IN HER SHOES

The purple Uggs sitting in my closet aren't mine.

My sweet mother-in-law bought these Uggs for my then 13-year-old daughter. She wanted them bad, but I didn't want to spend the money, so Grandma jumped in to save the day. She picked out her favorite color – purple – and sent them to her to open on her birthday.

My daughter wore these shoes all the time for six weeks. And then, seemingly overnight, her feet grew two sizes and no longer fit into her favorite comfy shoes.

So, when the cold weather came early this year, I saw the pair of purple boots sitting lonely in our coat closet. I thought about giving them away, but instead, I put them on and they fit my feet just right.

I wore them for a quick trip to the grocery store and to take the dog for a walk around the block. I wore them for carpooling and my dentist appointment. Sometimes I got looks from other people my age, probably wondering what a mid-40s woman was doing walking around in purple boots, but I also received compliments for the lovely color of my shoes.

And even though purple has never been my favorite color, I started feeling closer to my daughter every time I wore them. I almost felt like I understood her a little better by walking in her shoes.

I noticed that even though she grew four inches the past year, she still looked so small under the weight of her stuffed backpack. I imagined the weight she must feel and the stress of the books inside containing equations and Spanish vocabulary and novels that I read when I was much older.

I looked at the computer and phone and game system and iPad sitting around her – and recognized how hard it must be to stay focused and on task with all these technology distractions at her fingertips.

I saw her soccer cleats and running shoes and gym uniform, and instead of getting mad because they were scattered all over her room, I became amazed at her love for sports and how hard she works. She goes to early-morning practices and late-night games and never complains.

And I look down at these boots and think it must be tough to get something you love only to have it not fit one day when you go to put them on. How awkward must it be to try to adjust to a new body that seemingly changed overnight?

The start of the teen years in our house was rough, and I think sometimes I get so annoyed by her behavior that I lose a little bit of my compassion, too.

It's hard to ignore the messy rooms and the snarky comments and the emotional roller coaster we all have to ride with her some days.

But these boots are a great reminder that while there are so many changes I have to deal with as a parent to a teenager – that actually being a teenager can be pretty tough, too.

A few months later, I bought my daughter a new pair of boots for Christmas, but it was good for me to walk a mile in her shoes.

It may be good for you too.

55. A Word about the Empty Nest

I talked to a neighbor recently who is expecting her first grandchild soon. She excitedly told me about how her daughter was feeling and the anticipation of being grandparents. She gushed about her youngest, who recently graduated from college and is starting her new life. She talked about visiting her son.

She spoke about vacations she planned with friends and the fishing trip her husband just returned from and dinners with her sister. She told me about caring for a sick relative and volunteering at her church. She talked about books and movies and new restaurants.

Her life was full.

She asked about my girls and how they were faring in high school. I waited for the "It all goes so fast" or "Enjoy it while you can" commentary, but she didn't mention it.

Instead, she said something so profound: "There's always something to look forward to when you have a family."

Bam. Mic drop.

There's always something to look forward to when you have a family.

I'm at the time in my life when it all seems to be moving so fast. My girls are almost women, and their time under my roof is limited.

Yet, I still see a future for us, and I'm doing the work today to make sure they know I want to be in their life tomorrow.

But preparing for my birds to leave the nest means I have to prepare myself as well.

So, I've been trying to find what fuels my fire again, beyond caring for my children.

I'm working in a job that I love. I write. I cook. I volunteer with my kids. I'm spending more time alone with my husband.

I see a life – a rich, beautiful, full life – which grows in lockstep with my children, instead of centered around it.

There is always something to look forward to when you have a family. There is always something to look forward to when you have friends. There is always something to look forward to if you look at it in the right way.

My kids may no longer live underneath my roof, but the ties will not be fully cut.

There will be graduations and weddings and births. There will be vacations and celebrations and achievements. There will be times they need me to hold them up and take them in, and there will be times I need them to do the same.

There is still so much to look forward to, even though our lives will look different.

My nest may soon be empty, but I choose to believe that my life will still be full.

THE END

ACKNOWLEDGMENTS

There would be no book on my experiences raising teenagers if it were not for the three glorious creatures who call me "Mom." Thank you, Olivia, Camryn and Payton, for letting me share some of our stories with the world. You bring me so much joy.

I would also like to thank my dear friend Jill Gill for inviting me to her house for Friday playdates when our kids were in preschool. You showed me that vulnerability is a beautiful quality in friendship. Your support over the years and the love you have gifted our family will always be in my heart.

To the women in my life who constantly build me up, including my Gator girls, the Queenagers, my business partner Kira Lewis, and the online publishers who have taught me so much, thank you for believing in me and my words.

Thank you to my Whitney Fleming Writes social media community for constantly requesting and encouraging me to put this book together. I hope we continue to be an example of how social media can be used for good.

I would also like to thank my mom, Sally, for letting me talk her ear off over the years about the trials and tribulations of motherhood. Most of my best work came after our phone calls, and I hope you know what an amazing role model you have been to me in every way.

And to my husband, Mark. Thank you for walking beside me in this life, encouraging me to chase my dreams with every step. You will always be my favorite chapter.

ABOUT THE AUTHOR

W hitney Fleming is the co-owner of the *Parenting Teens & Tweens* blog and runs the popular social media accounts Whitney Fleming Writes. She believes that being vulnerable and sharing your story is the most powerful way we can help others, so she made a career out of it. She brings an authentic voice to topics such as raising teenagers, mid-life, marriage and mental health. Whitney resides in the suburbs of Chicago with her three beautiful daughters, her incredibly patient husband and her extremely disobedient dog, Jax.